HISTORIC DYES SERIES

No.3

MEDIEVAL TEXTILE DYEING

FIRST EDITION 2003

Copyright © remains the property of the publisher.

John Edmonds - Publisher

89 Chessfield Park, Little Chalfont, Bucks. HP6 6RX

John Edmonds

ISBN 0 9534133 2 2

Foreword

During the period from the 12th century to the 16th century, Italy experienced the first industrial revolution based on textile manufacture and trade in a wide variety of commodities. This in turn made possible the Italian cultural renaissance founded on the wealth generated by this expansion. In 16th century there was the expansion of Portugal, Spain, Holland, France and England into the New World and the Far East.

All Europe saw the development of craft guilds during this period, which improved standards of workmanship and training, but at the same time acted in restraint of trade by developing monopolies and restricting entry to the profession. On top of this were the exactions in terms of tolls, customs duties and plain and unfair extortion amounting to brigandage imposed by medieval kings, princes and magnates, plus wars and religious bigotry. In addition there was widespread piracy particularly in the Mediterranean Sea. In spite of this, Europe saw the foundations laid for future industrial expansion in terms of banking, insurance, financial futures and merchant law and ever increasing trade. The change in Europe from a feudal to a more emancipated society was driven as always by the growth of technology. This included the long bow, the invention of gunpowder and waterpower and the printing of books. A rising standard of living can be seen, using brickwork, chimneys and glazed windows in domestic buildings.

Intellectual developments from improved navigation to astronomy and scientific instruments followed these changes. This booklet is devoted to the art of the professional dyers in the years before 1600 and attempts to illustrate the methods used at that time. It becomes apparent that the methods developed empirically by the dyers were in general based on a remarkable understanding of the mordanting effects of soluble metal compounds, acids and alkalis, and tannins in fixing dyes to cloth and the results of mixing dyestuffs and the treatment of cloth. This was the result of acute observation unsupported by theory or scientific methodology. The use of bran and the fermentation of woad and Tyrian purple were biochemistry before the subject was invented. At the same time one is aware that some awful practices were used which would have been injurious to the health of the artisans. Arsenic, soluble lead and mercury compounds are not substances we are prepared to use today in textile dyeing. It is hoped that this booklet will assist in appreciating the developments, which have taken place in this craft.

CONTENTS

Illustrations 5
Logwood dyed on blue   1 5
Introduction 6
The transition from medieval to 18th century dyeing 9
The "Old and New Draperies" 17
Chaucers remarks on clothing and dyeing 19
The Sumptuary Laws 23
The early history of purple silk in Europe 26
Medieval Crafts in England 26
Bristol, London and Southampton 35
The Italian Cloth Trade 37
The Available dyes and mordants 40
Black 42
Blue 45
Painted Cloth 48
Standard methods of medieval dyeing 48
Dyer's Alkanet 51
Archil or Orchil 51
Brazilwood 54
Fenugreek (Trigonella foenum graecum) Greek Hay 55
Genista tinctoria or Dyer's Broom 55
Indigo 55
Imperial Purple 55
Kermes or Grain and Polish Cochineal 56
Madder 57
Persian Berries 57
Pomegranate 58
Saffron 58
Sticklac 59
Tannins 60
Oak galls 60
Sage 60
Weld 61
Woad 61

Young fustic 62
Mordant used in 1548 Italy in: - 62
Verdigris 63
Iron salts 63
Wood ash 63
Urine 64
Saltpetre 64
Alum 64
Pearl Ash 64
Bran 65
Conclusions 65
APPENDICES 66
1) 15th. century recipe for the woad vat 66
2) Ordinance of the Bristol Guild of Dyers in 1439 74
3) Act of Queen Elizabeth 1 prohibiting the use of logwood 1567 79
4) A proclamation prohibiting the export of wool except as finished cloth. 1606 82
5) Dyestuffs listed and used in 1548 in Italy 84
6) Chemicals in Medieval Dyeing 1448 85
7) Medieval Dye Recipes 87
No.1 Yellow 87
No. 2 Safflower 88
No.3 To make wool a light red 88
No 5 Blue 89
No 6 Green 89
No 7 Brown 89
No 8 Black wool 90
No 10 Brazilwood red 90
No 11 Red dyeing on thread, skeins, or linen 91

Illustrations

	Plate
Logwood dyed on blue	1
Medieval lead seals	2
Wool dyed with Kermes	3
Reds available before 1600	4
Yellow and Green	5
The woad plant in its first year	6
The Weld plant	7
The alum warehouse, Southampton	8

Introduction

An outline chronology[1] of the history of textiles and textile dyeing in Medieval Europe indicates the spread of this technology due primarily to the movement of skilled artisans. This was caused mainly by various forms of persecution and wars. In the early Middle Ages various tribes in Turkey and elsewhere in the Middle East, were skilled in the manufacture of carpets, towels, felted cloth and rugs. After 827 AD in Sicily after its conquest by the Arabs, high quality fabrics were made in the palace workshops in Palermo. In 1130, skilled weavers from Greece and Turkey came to Palermo and were producing silk fabrics containing gold threads.

In 1266, following the conquest of Sicily by the French, the weavers fled to Italy, many settling in Lucca which became famous for patterned silk fabrics.

In 1315, the Florentines captured Lucca, taking the Sicilian weavers to Florence, which was already a centre for fine woven woollen cloth since 1100. It is believed that in 1315 they were also manufacturing velvet in Florence. By the end of the 15th Century Florence employed some 16,000 workers in the silk industry and 30,000 in the manufacture of woollen fabrics.

From 1480 the textile industries of France and Germany were weaving silk. Francis 1 in 1520 brought Italian and Flemish weavers to Fontainebleu to manufacture tapestries. Other silk weavers were settled in Lyon, which became the European centre for silk manufacture. Until 1589 the most elaborate fabrics in France were of Italian origin. In 1589 Henry 1V of France founded the Royal carpet and tapestry factory at Savonnieres. And in the 16th century Flemish weavers were brought to France to produce tapestries in the factory set up by Jean Gobelin. Textile manufacture continued to advance up until it was interrupted by the French Revolution.

In England a similar trend can be seen, but much later. In the 13th and 14th centuries wool and linen were woven but much of it was finished abroad. In 1455 silk was woven in London and Norwich. In 1564 Queen Elizabeth 1 granted a charter to Dutch and Flemish settlers in Norwich to produce damasks and flowered silk. The revocation of the Edicts of Nantes in 1685 resulting in the renewed persecution of French Protestants caused many weavers to move to England, settling in Norwich, Braintree, and London. The biggest group, some 3,500 settled in Spitalfields in London and it became the centre for fine silk damasks and brocades.

The extent and sophistication of the textile dyeing industry in Britain and Europe at the time of the Norman conquest is difficult to assess. During the Roman occupation we know from archaeological evidence that the Roman Army had its own imperial dye works at Winchester and undoubtedly elsewhere. At Pompeii we have a wall painting depicting dyers at work. There is the imperial edict of the Roman emperor referring to woollen cloth imported from England. Pliny the Elder in his Natural History devotes several pages to textile dyeing including madder and of course the imperial purple. With the final demise of Roman authority in Western Europe, trade in everything including textiles rapidly declined. We have Saxon place names referring to woad, suggesting a widespread use of the dye and its cultivation. At York the Viking enclave at

Coppergate demonstrates the importance of textile dyeing in the 9th and 10th centuries.

Before the rise of the medieval guild, textile dyeing went unregulated and unrecorded. One indication of the extent of the manufacture and trade in textiles is the use of place names for various colours. For blue particularly, Watchett and Plunket were shades of blue. In Florence in the early 15th century there was a blue known as Turkish blue and another was Roman blue. Later there are references in England to Lincoln green and Kendal green.

Sadly the quantity of textiles of European origin, which have survived from the medieval period to the present day, is very small compared with later periods. Those we have range from the Bayeaux tapestry of the 11th century to wall tapestries of the 14th and 15th centuries, and various ecclesiastical garments. Cheap and inferior cloth such as the "burel" referred to in the literature is virtually non-existent except possibly for small scraps of rag preserved in graves and other archaeological deposits. It appears to have been a coarse loosely woollen weave, not dressed or subject to the complex finishing process or even dyed but having the appearance of sacking.

Wall tapestries, where the wefts were predominantly made of wool, are one of the forms of early textiles, which have survived and have been closely studied. There is a continuous history of tapestry manufacture in Europe. Tapestry has been defined[2] *as a fabric formed of threads, inserted by hand, passing alternatively in and out on the parallel strings of a warp stretched upon a frame or loom. The weft threads are not completely thrown across the loom, but are introduced to cover spaces with various colours and tints as required by the design. The warp is thus completely hidden in the finished fabric.* This definition dates to a time before the invention of computer controlled tapestry weaving. The establishment of a definite tapestry-making industry in Europe appears in the early 14th century A.D, although it originated in Egypt at a much earlier date. The earliest medieval tapestries contain some 12 to 15 hues and shades of colour. By the 15th century this had increased to 20 and even as many as 40. A tapestry made from a design of the period of Louis XIV is reputed to contain 79 colours. Tapestries of the 18th and 19th centuries tend to be finer with closer warps. Vast sums were spent on tapestries for wall hangings in prestigious buildings and even hired out for state and other festive occasions. High quality tapestries like other costly fabrics were normally purchased from Italy or Flanders. Even a series of tapestries to commemorate the defeat of the Spanish Armada was designed by a Dutchman and woven in the Netherlands. William Sheldon made the first attempt to establish a tapestry industry in England with an artisan trained in the Netherlands. The Mortlake tapestry factory was established in 1619 under the patronage of James 1, again with imported weavers from the continent. This establishment finally closed in 1703. Frequently the immigrant artisans were carefully vetted and required a certificate of residence stating *"Jan Gelison, dyer, Flanders. No fanatic. His conversation is honest."*

The transition from medieval to 18th century dyeing

It may seem perverse to introduce the subject of textile dyeing in medieval Europe by considering the changes, which occurred, in the 16th and 17th centuries. But there is a reason for this. We have so little direct historical information on dyeing before 1500 that we must to some degree, proceed backwards by deduction and circumstantial evidence if we are to form a picture of the medieval dye industry. We have ample evidence of later practices and we know of the improvements, which occurred in the 16th and early 17th. Centuries. From this, combined with the written evidence and archaeological finds, a picture emerges.

Two aspects need to be borne in mind. Firstly in Britain in particular there was an enormous change in the quality and availability of textiles between the largely homespun fabrics of the 11th. Century, produced on vertical looms and spun with drop spindles and the "new draperies" of the 17th. Century One can compare the so-called Bayeaux tapestry of wool embroidered on linen in about 1086, with the later tapestries and table carpets, velvets and "cloths of gold" and a whole range of lesser fabrics of the 16th century. The Bayeaux tapestry represents a very important document commissioned by a member of William the Conqueror's family and follows the tradition of the Saxon Broiderie Anglais or opus anglicanum, while the "new draperies" were available to anyone who could afford them.

Secondly, there is the enormous range of fabrics available in the later middle ages, largely imported from either Italy, France or Flanders, at a time when there was very little finished cloth exported from England. The only important export from England was raw wool, fels and fleeces, and unfinished woven cloth from which high quality fabrics were produced abroad. As late as 1630 three quarters of all the cloth exported to Germany and Holland was un-dyed and unfinished. The cloth increased 100% in value after dyeing and finishing.[3.1] The changing legislation in

England throughout this period reflects a growing concern with this state of affairs.

Another difficulty in summarising the dyeing techniques in the medieval period in Europe is the variety of techniques and sophistication which existed across Europe. In Italy and later in France, Flanders, and eventually in Britain high quality spinning, weaving, dyeing and finishing of cloth existed while at the same time, other areas were dependent on a cottage industry using locally grown fibres and using wild plant ingredients for dyeing homespun cloth. A parallel to this situation is very well illustrated by the experience of the early settlers in North America in the late 17th and 18th century. At that time British settlers were importing cloth of all qualities from Britain. At the same time German immigrants amongst others, were trying to build an indigenous textile industry based on locally grown linen and wool. They produced inferior textiles for their own use and for sale to the Indians in exchange for skins and furs. This small colonial industry closely followed the techniques German and other immigrants had learned before emigrating. The Indians appeared to produce very little textile and were wearing clothing made of skins and furs. These they were willing to exchange for cheap textiles from the settlers. William Penn included cloth as part of the purchase price for land purchased from the Indians in New England.

One of the most important dyestuffs of the medieval period, namely woad has been the subject of the first booklet in this series. However more research has in recent months been completed and these results are given in the section on woad in this booklet. In addition the opportunity has been taken to repeat in full the medieval recipe for woad dyeing dated 1418. This was recovered from the guild archives in Florence and translated by Dr Dominique Cardon, who has very kindly given permission to include it in this booklet. The recipe was not originally intended to be published but was a secret document of the guild to be used for the instruction of the guild apprentices. The recipe therefore assumes some knowledge and experience of the woad vat. It is hoped that the explanation of medieval woad dyeing given in the first booklet in this series will supply the background required.

Very little was written by practising dyers recording their art in the Middle Ages. All over Europe the dyers' craft like most others, was closely controlled by the guilds. An apprenticeship was the only way to learn the craft, and apprentices were controlled by the guilds. Nevertheless, although new dyestuffs and mordants became available by 1600, and others went out of use, the basic techniques for handling and dyeing wool remained virtually unchanged over many centuries.

One great distinction between the practices of textile dyeing in Europe before the 16th Century and that occurring later is apparent. The common dyestuffs available in Europe before the economic watershed of the 16th century were in general those which were indigenous to Europe or could be cultivated there. Others were available such as indigo and brazilwood and turmeric from the East, but these were not in common use in dyeing, except possibly in Italy. After this date America had been discovered and the sea routes to India and the Far East were open. The various tropical plant dyes such as logwood, annatto, brazilwood and the cochineal insect were now commonly available from Central

America, and Indigo and Sticklac from India. In 1607 the scarlet achieved with cochineal and tin chloride had been discovered. Not only were new colours now available more cheaply but the dyers were also able to improve their techniques.

Surprisingly we have a reference to the use of a tin vessel in Plictho[3] of 1548 as follows:-

168 To make a water that restores the colour to cloths of silk and of all sorts that are faded.

Take for each five parts of common water one part of soda ash well pestled. Put into a tin pot on the fire and leave it to boil well until it has raised the boil. Then strain it and let it cool. When you want to use it make it a little tepid and wash the stains and let them dry. When they are dry, if they are a little lighter than the other places, wet the stains with wine, and return to wet them with the said water and let them dry. If they are too dark add to the wine a little common water and go treating according to the need, whether lighter or darker, as many times until you find the colour perfect. And this is the rule.

It is possible that tin in some form as a mordant, was used in Venice to produce red.

In the early medieval period the quality of cloth produced in England was so poor that there was virtually no export of cloth except as a raw material for reworking. Only the English wool clip, "un-wrought" in the form of fleeces and fels (wool still on the skins) was in great demand. In Italy at the same time high quality cloth of wool, silk and linen and even cotton were in production. These were exported to the whole of Europe. Exotic dyestuffs and mordants were imported into Italy, such as alum, indigo, sticklac and turmeric, and realgar and orpiment, which are compounds of arsenic which were used in dyeing and were mined as minerals in the Red Sea region and in India. Italy had a monopoly of the alum trade from Turkey and later when it was also mined in Italy. Cotton was imported into Italy at a time when it was virtually unknown in the rest of Europe. Cotton textiles were not produced and printed in England until about 1750. The Italian textiles, spices, silks and works of art were in demand all over Europe. The point remains valid however that these were not available to the majority of the population of Western Europe. Apart from the cost, the use of crimson and scarlet were confined to the aristocracy by the sumptuary laws. Most of the dyestuffs used earlier were still in use after 1600 but by then the exotic dyes were freely available and these were combined in new recipes.

Flanders became a centre of high quality textile as well as regions of France. Finally as a result of religious persecution and politics, refugees brought the art of textile manufacture to England which in turn by 1600 was becoming a leading textile manufacturer.

One very valuable book, The Plictho[3], was published in 1548, not, regrettably, by a practising dyer, but by an influential man of those times namely Gioanventura Rossetti. He is described as the provisioner of the Arsenal in Venice. He was clearly interested in dyeing textiles, leather and feathers, etc. and had the money and influence to obtain recipes and information from the dyers. The problem is however to tease out the relevant facts from his book. Unfortunately this book was written in the late medieval period. It comes at a time of transition from dependence on mainly plants and beetles of European origin to those dyestuffs such as annatto and brazilwood and indigo obtained from tropical regions. This followed as a result of the discovery of America and the sea routes to the East.

Rossetti enlarges on the secrecy of the trade and his reason for publishing. He states *"You must know that this is a work of charity that I bequeath for the public benefit, and which has been imprisoned for a great number of years in the tyrannical hands of those who kept it hidden."*

It is questionable whether Rossetti's recipes reflect the common dyeing practices of the rest of Europe. Italy lay at the centre of trade between the East and the rest of Europe and for a long period Italy was the commercial and industrial hub of Europe. Geoffrey Chaucer in the 14th century refers to madder, weld and woad as the common ingredients for textile dyeing. Many local plants or lichens were used for homespun cloth and for the more affluent the second-hand clothes markets would have reflected the quality of imported fabrics worn by the very rich. There was considerable trade in second-hand clothes, which no doubt facilitated the spread of fleas and the plague. Fairs and markets attended by foreign merchants were held regularly in Bruges, Winchester and certainly in many other centres of population. Hygiene was not a consideration at that time, but clothes were washed and reworked to make them look new, thus increasing their attractiveness and value.

The records of the very prosperous Italian merchant from Prato, Francesco di Marco Datini[4] (1334 -1410), a contemporary of Chaucer's, indicate the importance and sophistication of the textile trade in Italy. Francesco himself, as a merchant in textiles, was a member of the cloth guild of the Arte della Lana, in Florence, although he traded in many other commodities. A separate and skilled operative would carry out each stage in the processing and finishing of cloth. These were the washers, carders, spinners, warpers, weavers, dyers, fullers, clippers, menders and folders. Not only were the pay and working conditions controlled by the guild but even the operative's religious observances. The master dyer was commonly known as the tintore di guado or woad dyer. The woad vat required the greatest skill and experience. Among the commodities in which Francesco traded were, saffron, alum, woad, orchil, kermes, indigo, Indian lac, orpiment (arsenic sulphide), galls (tannin), red and white tartar, gum arabic, Valencia soap, and wool as well as bales of finished cloth. The local Italian wool was apparently used for coarse cheap cloth. Spanish, African, Minorcan, Provencale or English wool was preferred. English wool from the Cotswolds (Chondisgualdo) was in great demand. It was collected from places such as Northleach (Norleccio), Burford (Boriforte), Cirencester (Sirisestri) and Winchester (Guincestri).

The reason why English wool in the Middle Ages was so highly regarded in Europe is not obvious. Today there appears to be every type of wool produced in England from coarse long staple suitable for carpets to the fine short wool depending on the breed. The most likely explanation is that given by Professor Charles Wilson[5] who states that the wool from the midlands and southern England before the 16th century was a fine short staple produced on unimproved pastures while after this period richer grazing resulted in a coarser wool. Certainly after this period the renowned Cotswold wool was replaced with the fine merino wool, originally from Spain. The changing market in England and on the continent further compounds the picture, which by

1650 was increasingly for long staple wool for worsted, stuffs and kerseys.

The "Old and New Draperies"

For the purpose of this study we have neatly divided history into medieval and modern by the arbitrary date of 1600. The change however was much more gradual than this implies. The way of life and social attitudes was still essentially medieval in England long after 1600. The change from the "old" to the "new" draperies is a case in point. This occurred in the first half of the 17th century. This change not only marked a shift in the type of fabrics in demand, but a change in the places of cloth manufacture. There was a change of the operatives employed, and was marked by a social change from heavy woollen garments to lighter clothes. More attractive worsted apparel and furnishing fabrics were coming into fashion both in England and abroad.

The same problem occurs with identifying these fabrics from their names as in identifying colours from names such as Lincoln or Kendal green or the plunkets, watchets and drabs. Professor C. Wilson in his book The Apprenticeship of England published in 1957 gives a very useful lead. We must pick our way through the jerseys, bays and says and the *"divers broad Clothes, Kersies, Woolls, Pennestones, Bayes, Cottons, Hose, Yarn, Hats, Caps, Flannels, Dockadoes, Rashes, tuft Dockadoes, and other things,"* enshrined in Elizabethan statutes.

It appears that the old draperies were basically heavy woollen cloth using short staple fine carded wool, which today would be used for woollen blankets and baize cloth. Kersies were a cheap roughish woollen cloth with the weave visible to the eye. Burel was an even cheaper and coarser woollen cloth, with a loosely woven tabby weave.

The New Draperies were lighter, brighter and cheaper and more fashionable. Amongst these were the following fabrics: -

East Anglian stuffs – long staple combed worsted cloth. Others were bays, says, perpetuanos, shaloon, grosgrain and serge.

Say was a hard wearing worsted, used for men's dress, monk's shirts in Italy and Spain, and in a green version for Quaker's aprons.

Bays – a Colchester speciality – a kind of coarse open woollen stuff – exported in considerable quantities to Spain, Portugal and Italy for monks and nuns and as a lining for military uniforms. Also used behind mirrors to preserve the tin and quicksilver coating.

Perpetuanos – not unlike says and made in Suffolk.

Callimancoes – a light worsted in striped colours much in favour with the Eastland merchants. They sold well in Russia where the Tartar and Siberian tribes were said to use them for sashes.

Baytrie or goods of the bay type

Bombazines bright stuff often made of a mixture of wool and silk – an early imitation of Indian fabrics.

Serges something like bays and says but somewhat heavier, and the type known as "perpetuana" advertised their durability. Their strength was due to two different types of wool – a fine short woollen weft later imported from Spain and a worsted wool warp.

Spanish cloth was the name given to woollen cloth made from imported Spanish merino wool dyed and finished in Wiltshire and Somerset with stammels or scarlet in the

Stroudwater district of Gloucestershire This was probably the fore runner of Victorian broadcloth.

The New Draperies originated in Flanders and the technique was introduced into England by the influx of Flemish refugees many of whom were skilled textile workers. Professor Wilson gives a 17th century Dutch estimate of the cost of manufacturing woollen cloth: -

	Percentage costs
Raw material	10
Combing	6
Spinning	2
Weaving	7
Fulling	5
Dyeing	47
Miscellaneous	10
Profit	13
Total	100

The value of the cloth is more than doubled by the fulling and dyeing. The New Draperies and new imported dyestuffs and improved methods of the 17th century mark the transition from medieval to 18th century natural dye industry. This was again transformed 200 years later with the introduction of synthetic dyes.

Chaucers remarks on clothing and dyeing

Geoffrey Chaucer (c.1340-1400)[6] is a primary source of evidence for clothing and social customs in the 14th Century. He describes in detail the clothing worn by the pilgrims each attired according to the custom of his guild and his station in life. Descriptions of men and women's attire are also given in the tales told by these same pilgrims. The quality of the clothing immediately indicates the affluence of the wearer. In one of his shorter poems, "The Former Age", Chaucer speculates on a mythical golden age when no one was vain and every one wore un-dyed woollen clothes, that remained the colour of the fleece and when dyers knew nothing of "mader, weld or wode". These were the common dyestuffs, grown as field crops, available to commercial dyers in Britain, giving a brick red, yellow and blue. Browns and blacks were commonly achieved with iron salts and tannin. The craft of dyeing in fact, seems to be as old as textiles themselves.

In a passage in the Parsons Tale the seven deadly sins are dealt with in detail and pride in ostentatious garments is singled out for censure. This gives us an insight at least into ecclesiastical attitudes into contemporary fashions of the period: -

"But nevertheless that one of these species of pride is a sign of that other, just as the gay bush on the tavern wall is a sign of the wine in the cellar. And this is in many things: as in speech and countenance, and in the outrageous display of clothing. For certainly if there had been no sin in clothing, Christ would not so soon have noted and spoken of the clothing of the rich man in the Gospels. And as St Gregory said, "precious clothing is culpable for the costliness of it, and for its softness and for its exotic style and elaborateness and for its superfluity and for its scantiness."

Alas, may men not see, as in our day, the sinful costly display of clothing and namely in too much superfluity or else in excessive scantiness?

As to the first sin, that is in the superfluity of clothing, which makes it so dear to the harm of people; not only the cost of embroidery, ostentatious notching of the border cloth dyed one colour, vertical stripes or decorative borders, and similar waste of cloth in vanity, but there is also the costly fur trimmings in their gowns, so much punching designs with ornamental holes, so much slitting with shears; furthermore with the superfluity in length of the aforesaid gowns, trailing in the dung and in the mire, on horse and also on foot, as well of man as of woman, that all this tailoring is verily in effect wasted, consumed, threadbare and rotten with dung, rather than it is given to the poor, to the great damage of the aforesaid poor folk, it is not convenient to wear for their estate, nor sufficient to meet their need, to protect them from inclement weather. Upon the otherside to speak of the horribly inordinate scantiness of clothing, as are those loose short outer tunics, or haynselyns, that through their shortness do not cover the shameful members of a man, to wicked intent. Alas, some of them show the bulge of their chap, and the horrible swollen members, that seem like the malady of hernia, in the wrapping of their hose; and also the buttocks of them fare as it were the hind part of a she-ape in the full moon. And more over, the wretched swollen members that show through their style of clothing, in dividing their hose in white and red, it seems that half their shameful privee members were flailed. And if it is that they divide their hose in other colours, such as white and black, or white and blue or black and red as by variation of the colour it appears that half their privee members were corrupted by the fire of St Antony, or by cancer, or by some other mischance. Of the hind part of their buttocks, it is quite horrible to see. For certainly in that part of their body where they purge their stinking ordure, that foul part they show proudly to the people in spite of honesty, which honesty that Jesus Christ and his friends observed to show in their lives. Now as to the outrageous display of women, God knows that though the faces of some of them are full chaste and gracious, yet in their attire they display lechery and pride. I do not say that honest clothing of man and woman is unseemly, but certainly the superfluity or inordinate scantiness of clothing is reprehensible. Also the sin of ornament is in things which appertain to riding, as in many delicate horses that are kept for pleasure that are so handsome, fat and costly; and also in the many vicious knaves that are sustained because of them; and in too curious harness, as in saddles, in covers for the hind quarters of horses, horse collars and bridles covered with precious cloth, and rich bars and plates of gold and silver. For which God said by Zechariah the prophet, "I will confound the riders of such horses." These folk take little notice of the riding of God's son of heaven, and of his harness when he rode upon an ass, and had no other harness but the poor clothing of his disciples; we do not read that he rode on any other beast. I say this for the sin of superfluity, and not for reasonable honesty, when reason requires it. And furthermore certainly pride is greatly made known in the holding of a great many when they are of little profit or no profit, and namely when that many is felonious and dangerous to the people by hardiness of high lords or by way of offices. For certainly such lords sell more than their lordships to the devil in hell, when they sustain the wickedness of their households. Or else when this folk of low degree as keep hostelries, sustain the theft of the hostellers and that in many kinds of deceit. These kinds of people are like flies that follow the honey, or else like hounds that follow carrion."

In the epilogue to the Nun's Priest Tale, Chaucer mentions "brasile ne with greyn of Portyngale". Brasilwood for dyeing was imported from the Far East as a red dye and grain was the kermes insect. Both of these were very expensive dyes reserved for the wealthy.

One of the clerks in the Miller's Tale is clad "in a kirtle of light waget"- watchet was a light blue that presumably originated in the village of Watchet.

The Sumptuary Laws

In most of Europe including Britain, the so-called Sumptuary Laws were enacted at various times throughout the Middle Ages. In England they remained on the statute book from 1337 to 1604, and in Poland as late as 1776. These restricted the colours, materials and even the types of garments, that various classes of society were permitted to wear. Normally the very expensive colours such as crimson and scarlet were reserved for the nobility. Similarly when long toed shoes were fashionable, the length was restricted for all lower classes of persons. In Italy maidservants were not allowed to wear hats, high-heeled shoes or gilt or silver buttons. The justification given for these restrictions was to reduce expenditure on unnecessary luxury and sinful pride, but the effect, if not the purpose was to clearly differentiate the upper classes from the plebeians. The apparel was meant to proclaim the man. Cost alone would have ensured this distinction but as with most absurd and intrusive laws, it was more honoured in the breach than in its observance. Craftsman generally would wear their working overalls, as badges of guild membership like freemasons. Chaucer's pilgrims in the Canterbury Tales were remarkably well dressed but nevertheless their trades or social standing were clearly recognisable. Servants and retainers would expect to be clothed in various liveries at their master's expense, while those of higher social standing were given expensive garments, in recognition of services rendered. Chaucer himself frequently received gifts of clothing. At the other end of the social scale, paupers, almsmen and the deserving poor were also given clothing suitable to their station in life.

The abolition of the Sumptuary laws in England came about in 1604 not because of some new enlightenment but simply because the King, Lords and Parliament could not agree on who should be included. The King wanted sartorial privilege to be restricted to the Royal family, the Lords wanted to include the nobility and the Commons wanted it extended to the landed gentry.

Of course by today's standards all textiles at that time were incredibly expensive, even the poorest garments were of necessity, hand made and hand sown. Clothes were frequently stolen; the dead and dyeing on the battlefield were stripped of their garments and all clothes went down the social scale to become finally rags worn by the beggar. It seems very probable that most of the population in the Middle Ages would have been wearing second-hand clothes. There were international fairs and markets both in England and the rest of Europe for second-hand garments. It was in about 1813 that the shoddy industry was established in Batley in Yorkshire when a machine was devised to convert discarded garments back into wool fibre. The wool was then re-spun and woven into reconditioned cloth later known as "heavy woollen". It seems that the last manifestation of shoddy was as late as 1960 when army greatcoats were still made from this material. People were frequently buried in cheap pseudo clothes, adequate only for the sake of appearances. The Act of Parliament in England requiring every one to be buried in woollen shrouds was in force from 1666 to 1814. This particular piece of legislation was unique to England and was intended simply to increase the demand for woollen cloth and discourage the import of continental linen, which was the preferred fabric for this purpose. The act even stipulated that wool was to be used to line the coffin or for any outer covering. The penalty for contravening the act was £5 and remained the same throughout the 148 years of its existence. A certificate was required from the officiating clergyman to certify the act was applied at each funeral. An informer reporting any contravention was entitled to a reward of £2.50. For those families determined to ignore the act it was the practice for a member of the family to act as informer thus in effect reducing the fine to £2.50.

After 1669 the export of woolfels, fleeces and all unwrought wool was once again made legal.

Clothes were frequently restored by re-dyeing. Another use for discarded textiles was in papermaking. As late as the nineteenth century there were complaints from the residents of Windsor Castle objecting to the appalling smell of old rags being transported by barge up the River Thames to be reworked into paper at High Wycombe. The word frippery derives from the old French word meaning rags.

There was a trade in which the workers were known as the fripperers.

The early history of purple silk in Europe

The silk route from China to Persia existed as early as 114 BC[7]. Silk has however been found at Palmyra dating to before 272 BC when the city was destroyed. Tyre and Beirut in the Lebanon were at the western end of the silk route and were the centres for imperial purple dyeing and where the silk could be dyed. Constantinople was only able to compete with these centres after the introduction of sericulture by Justinian. By 330 AD, the time of Constantine the Great chose Constantinople as his capital it became the main centre for the production and distribution of silk cloth. In 424 AD Theodosius 11 banned the production of purple silk by private enterprise.

Medieval Crafts in England

From the point of view of the consumer, quality control and restrictive practices in trade and industry represented the acceptable and unacceptable aspects of regulation. In Medieval Britain as in the rest of Europe everything was closely controlled. Most public activities, such as fairs, importing and exporting, mining and establishment of companies and guilds required royal approval or at least acquiescence. This would usually be by charter or by decree. The guilds, livery companies and local corporations of cities or boroughs in turn controlled all the activities of its members or inhabitants with bylaws sanctioned by their charters. The number of apprentices allowed, their lives and working conditions and length of apprenticeship, the licensing of journeymen to practice their trade in a given place and the periodic inspection of their work and rates of remuneration were all aspects subject to control.

In the period 1200-1400 burels, russets, streits, worsteds and whites and chalons were produced. These were woollen cloths of poor coarse quality, sometimes fulled. The wool would have been from the short wool and woven in Colchester, Winchester and probably elsewhere. A superior cloth was worsted, also produced during this period, using a longer staple.

Woodger working from the Winchester Customs of 1275 maintains there were two guilds of cloth workers in Winchester, the burel weavers called telers and the chalon makers called tapeners. The chalon looms were of two types, single and double to produce blankets and quilts which were a double fabric. It is also suggested that burel was woven on looms presumably adapted from upright warp-weighted looms while the chalon weavers were using a two beam horizontal loom. The double cloth was woven by two weavers sitting beside each other, allowing much wider cloth to be made. By the end of the 13th century the English weavers were in competition with the Flemish weavers who were using broad horizontal looms which worked faster and produced a superior cloth.

The dyers in particular were in a very weak position and were subject to three main restraints; firstly their activities were closely controlled by their guilds, secondly their customers were the, mercers, haberdashers and cloth merchants who were themselves in stronger guilds and could dictate their requirements. Finally there were at various times the sumptuary laws restricting the colours and fashions each class in society could wear. In addition there was very strong international competition, first from Italy and then from France and Flanders. The aristocratic class in England as elsewhere wanted the very best fabrics and to get them they allowed the free importation of silks, quality woollen and linen fabrics. In the first half of the Middle Ages there was virtually no established business community in England comparable with those abroad except for the export of wool fleeces and fels. In any case, all customs and later, excise duties were within the royal prerogative and their imposition did not require parliamentary approval. One result was that different groups of merchants could be charged different rates of duties. Aliens and denizens were charged different rates and were subject to a number of petty restrictions. Surprisingly the German Hanse League (a powerful combination and brotherhood of German merchants) were at one time subject to lower rates of duties on the import and export of goods into England than were native English merchants. These favourable terms were in recompense for financial favours given to the King and donations to the city of London and presumably other corporations

All this militated against establishing a strong textile industry in England to compete with foreign quality products. English fleeces were normally exported, since the knowledge to produce high quality textiles did not exist in England. After 1350 the situation began to change as a result of the immigration from Europe into England of skilled artisans. This was actively encouraged by the English government and was later given a positive impulse as a result of religious and political persecution in Europe. Finally the export of "unwrought" wool from England except as cloth was banned, in order to assist the new textile industry.

One method used to ensure the quality of textiles was the use of lead seals attached to the lengths of cloth. The stamp on the lead seal indicated that the guild inspectors had passed the material. Many of these seals have been found in excavations of the medieval London quays and a collection of them exists in the Museum of London. Seals could be attached for other purposes such as to show tax had been paid or the method of dyeing that had been used.

In most towns no one could practice certain crafts without being a member of the guild and usually a freeman of that town. An indentured apprenticeship was an essential qualification and this necessitated finding a guildsman to act as master who would be responsible for training the apprentice usually for a fee. The apprentice would normally become a member of the master's household and be totally under his control. There are stories of regulations that the London apprentices should not be fed salmon more than twice a week. Salmon was presumably a cheap food fished out of the River Thames. After usually a seven year apprenticeship and having reached the required standard of proficiency, the apprentice became a journeyman employed in that trade. However many apprentices did not complete their apprenticeships. The Merchant Taylors Company would not allow such persons to make new garments. It was however possible for them to alter or remake second-hand clothes. This would have provided employment for many drop out apprentices.

The guilds were frequently very influential in their locality and they would be supported by local byelaws enacted by town councils. The guildsmen in Chaucer's Canterbury Tales are depicted as prosperous burgesses. Land and money was frequently bequeathed to the Guilds by successful guild members. These acts of charity were to assist less fortunate brethren. Considerable amounts of property in London belonged to the livery companies, the rents and leases providing a substantial income. The accumulation of this wealth is presumably still the source of income of the London Livery companies.

In Britain, during the greater part of the Middle Ages, virtually all high quality cloth was imported. The dominant export was wool and wool fels unwashed, unspun and undyed. One type of English cloth referred to in the records was burel. The word is also used by Chaucer to denote a rough ill educated man. Burel was a cheap cloth, woven and sometimes dyed. and presumably looked like sacking. There was an export of inferior woollen cloth presumably burel, which was reworked by a specialist guild in Florence in Italy. There the cloth was brayed (scoured with hog's dung and human urine to remove the oil and size used in spinning and weaving), and then fulled, stretched and rinsed in fresh water, then if necessary cleaned with fullers earth. With all grease removed the cloth was then washed with soap and probably using rain water or soft water. Then it was tentered and dried. At some stage the cloth was remordanted and redyed, and rinsed again after dyeing. The nap of the cloth would be raised with teasels, sheared and blemishes removed, then brushed and oiled with odourless oil and even scented. Finally the cloth was dressed, pressed, folded and packed in paper or canvas. All these processes involved considerable labour and skill. Much of this cloth was then re-exported, some of it returned to England as superior cloth at a superior price.

Professor Franco Brunello in his monumental book –The Art of Dyeing in the history of Mankind published in 1973 gives an inventory of the contents of an Italian dye house in Prato in 1394. This belonged to Nicolo di Piero, a prosperous dyer in that city. The items included were:-

Two walled (built in) *frames, with six walled boilers, with six vats for dyeing, also walled, with three blocks for cleaning cloth.*
Prato woad
Ashes for dye baths (Potassium carbonate for use as an alkali).
Alum
Madder roots
Alder bark, nut tree bark (tannins)
Baskets and panniers for wool washing
Old nets, some good, some in bad condition.
Two tubs and two pails to weigh ashes.
Twenty empty woad sacks, some good, some on bad condition.
Six washboards for grand teint.
Three throwing machines for grand teint, with double water jets.
A tub for dye baths.
Three pails for adding water to dye baths.
A small sieve for fishing the wool out of the boilers.
Two walled in winches and one pulley, a cord and a hook with some iron chain.
One sieve in poor condition for sifting ashes.
Six covers of ordinary cloth to put over the vats.

One chest with two locks and a little writing table.
Six wooden vat covers and two tables to put near the canal for washing cloth.
One tub for holding washing ashes.
One large iron scale for weighing, that weighs four hundred pounds
One small scale, that weighs eighty three pounds.
One tin ink stand with penknife.
One old pitchfork, and various sticks for dye baths.
An old pine table for preparing cloth.
Two small forks and a scraper for the fire boxes of the boilers.
One iron shovel and a wooden one for ashes.
One cover of old panels for the boiler to place over the dye baths.

From this description this was primarily a woad dye house for dyeing both un-spun wool in the fleece and woollen cloth.

Brunello also gives a detailed description of the method for handling the fleeces during dyeing. This is from a treatise – Codex Riccardino No.2580 in the Riccardiana Library in Florence dating to the 15th century:-

They shape the wool into a kind of fleece and put this into a bag. Then they send it to the dyers, tying the bags by means of a chain to the rope hoist. They immerse it in the boiling water of a cauldron and leave it to boil for half an hour, then with the hoist haul out the sack and let it drain over the cauldron.

After draining, according to the colour desired, either nut, violet or blue, the wool is divided between two vats of very hot woad. In each cauldron they put twenty-five pounds and leave it there for 1/8 hour, putting in ashes, and madder water or whatever else is necessary for the preparation of the bath. Then they pull up the wool with hooks and sticks and squeeze it with their hands. When it is squeezed out they place it in two barrels one for each vat, or for each sack of wool its vat, and make two turns with the pole. To each barrel is assigned a boy to loosen the wool, that is to open it out and unravel the knots for spreading it. They remove the wool using an appropriately constructed net of ropes.

After the unravelling, the workers wash the wool in the dyer's well. They wash it in baskets, passing it from basket to basket and pressing it with their feet once or twice to drive out the water. When the wool is washed, they place it in a cauldron filled with boiling water and leave it for an 1/8 hour, and replace it in sacks as before. They raise the sacks with chains to drain the wool, place it again in the vats, as before, but changing the vats, so that the colour between the two vats will be equal. After an 1/8 hour stay in the vats and after a second turn sequence, using sticks, they hoist, the fibres of wool are collected from the vats with a net and several persons are put to unravelling it. After this, the workmen re-bag the wool and carry it to the (River) *Arno where it is washed basket to basket.*

Light blue cloth is placed in the vats like the dark blue, and they place them in sacks, one for each vat, where they keep them for 1/8 hour and dye them for a "turn" and a half. The bright blues for one "turn". For the first two, however they do keep them longer. And for the last, the wool is placed so that it will be darker. This is done in order to use every part of the woad that is left in it.

When the wool is washed, they send it outside to dry over racks. Then when it is returned to the dye works, they place it on a table for sorting. They remove the rough parts and the badly dyed pieces. Then they weigh it into seven pound sections and send it to the beater to be treated because during the dyeing it has become somewhat felted.

One must however treat these contemporary descriptions with a certain caution. It is apparent to any one who has dyed successfully using the medieval woad vat that this description has been written by an interested by-stander with little or no explanation from the dyer. Brunello himself accepts the description uncritically. No way is unspun wool "immersed in boiling water of a cauldron and leave it boil for half an hour, then with the hoist haul out...." The technique has always been to add the wool to warm water and then gradually raise to a gentle simmer. Then the vat is allowed to cool before removing the wool. To achieve nut or violet colour the wool would be first or subsequently dyed separately in another vat with tannins and iron salts or in a red vat for the violet.

The various ingredients of madder and ashes were added first to the woad vat to bring about the fermentation necessary to dissolve the indigo from the woad. This normally took about three days. Only when the indigo had been dissolved in the alkaline liquor at 50°C was the vat ready for the wool. The references to repeated "unraveling" of the wool and beating to open the fleece is interesting since it was essential that the wool was not felted if it was to be spun. Woad of good quality was always expensive. The dyers would dye to various shades of blue to exhaust the vats of their colour as efficiently as possible.

Bristol, London and Southampton

London, Southampton and Bristol were the three major ports for importing dyestuffs and textiles, surpassing Ipswich, Boston and Kings Lynn and each possessed districts devoted to textile dyeing. Bristol became one of the leading ports for the export of cloth in the early 14th century {British Museum Occasional Paper 93}

Customs and excise were usually paid at the city gates. Geoffrey Chaucer, apart from the literary masterpieces he wrote in his spare time, was controller of customs responsible for collection of the duty on the export of wool, sheepskins and leather through the port of London for twelve years from 1374. His dwellings at that time were conveniently arranged over the city gate on the city wall at Aldgate. This was a few minutes walk from the customs house. His salary was ten pounds per annum. The duty on wool was the principle royal revenue and paid the cost of foreign campaigns. The actual collection of customs was farmed out to rich merchants conversant with the trade. The controller's responsibility was to maintain separate rolls in his own hand as a check on the honesty of the collectors.

Bristol was soon overshadowed by London and Southampton. The Port Books of Southampton detail the imports entering Southampton during part of the 15th century. For Southampton we know that wine, woad and weld (a yellow dyestuff), in that order, were the three most important imports entering the port of Southampton at that time. Wool was apparently the main export. For London the evidence for the textile trade and dyeing is more indirect. As a result of extensive archaeological excavation on the Thames water-front between Queenshithe and London

Bridge considerable evidence has come to light. This illustrates the importance of London for the import, export and manufacture of textiles over a period of some 500 years from the the 13th to the 18th centuries.

The Vintry and Downgate wards on the north bank of the Thames between Queenshithe and London Bridge were at the heart of the City of London and at the centre of London's medieval trade. The Steelyard was in Vintry ward as the main factory of the Hansa League with its own quay, cranes, weigh-bridge and warehouses. The guildhall of the Worhipful Company of Dyers was originally in Downgate Ward overlooking the river. It was founded in about 1426 in the reign of Henry V1.

John Stow in his Survey of London quotes amongst other items from the accounts of the expenditure of the Earl of Lancaster at Christmas 1314 :-

2   cloths of scarlet for the Earl
1   cloth of russet for the Bishop of Agnew
70 cloths of blue for the knights
5   cloths of medley for the lord's clerks
4   cloths for minstrels and carpenters
7   hoods of purple
64 cloths saffron coloured for barons and knights
12 red cloths mixed
100 pieces of green silk for the knights
14 lamb skin furs for clerks
168 yards of russet cloth
24 coats for poor men with maundy money

The Italian Cloth Trade

The Italians were the first to dominate the cloth trade in Europe. Later the baton past to Flanders and northern France and finally to England. Most of the accessible information on medieval trade and textile manufacture in particular comes from Italian sources. Excellent records were kept by the guilds and the various merchants, and information has survived in Italian archives. In an illiterate age, the merchants ledgers were documents of great legal and commercial importance and were treated as family heirlooms. The Italians invented double entry book keeping, and maintained a network of factors, notaries, accountants and messengers travelling to branch offices throughout most of Europe. The sea routes from the Levant to Venice and Genoa across the Mediterranean Sea and around Spain to France, Flanders and England were dominated by Italian shipping. The first banking system was established by Italian Merchants. Italy at that time consisted of a number of sovereign states and free cities each competing with the other. The business letters and ledgers of a merchant of Prato in Tuscany have survived and much of the information published[8]. The Plictho of 1548 published in Venice gives details of a number of dye recipes used at that time. In England we have various guild records and decrees and acts of Parliament regulating the trade.

Trade with the Hanseatic

rly in northern Germany and centred on Lübeck with outposts or trading centres all over northern Europe and Britain. A rather jaundiced description of the league was written probably in the 18th century by an unknown English writer :-

THE LEAGUE

It is shameful that merchants should rule over high born and noble men, was a familiar complaint as medieval German traders known as Hansards wrested power from their noble Rulers in the thirteenth century. United for protection and profit, they used boycotts and occasional force to monopolise markets run from Hanseatic Towns and outposts throughout the Baltic and North Sea regions. By the 1600s when Hanseatic sea power had been eclipsed by the Dutch, the league was in decline.

From the Steelyard, a privileged enclave on the Thames near London Bridge, the Hansards exported English wool while importing wine from the Rhineland and finished textiles from Bruges. Bruges, site of the Hansards most important foreign outpost, was the centre of the Flemish textile market. To the east, German speaking League towns lined the lower Rhine.

Barrier to Hanseatic control over vital shipping lanes, an imperious Denmark was brought to heel in the war of 1361-69.

The presence of Hansards in Norway, from the arrival of merchants in the 1200s to the departure of the last "secretary" in 1761, outlasted the league itself by a century.

The port of Visby in Gotland in the Baltic Sea – entrepot for goods from east to west – grew rich early as the league's strategic Baltic stronghold. It declined in the 1300s as the Hansards used larger ships.

For decades Polish grain poured through the port of Danzig into Hanseatic ships. Behind the shields of the Teutonic knights, the Hansards thrust eastward into the

realms of the Poles and the Balts, establishing German ports from Danzig to Reval (Tallinn).
Hub for Russian furs and exotic goods from as far away as China, Novgorod played much the same role for the Hansards as it had earlier for Viking river traders.

The Hansa league was indeed a very rich and influential international trading corporation from 1241 to the early 17th century. It was formed originally as a protective union of German merchants against the brigandage and extortionate levies of the various princes and nobles in Germany. It then came to dominate trade in Northern Europe in the same way that Italian merchants dominated trade in Southern and Central Europe. Over 100 towns in Germany were at one time members of the league. In Britain their main warehouse or "factory" was at the Steelyard in Dowgate Ward near London Bridge with its own wharf on the Thames. Other factories were situated at Kings Lynn and even in the Shetland Isles with other outposts at Bristol, Norwich, Ipswich, Yarmouth, Boston, Hull and York.

Henry III, granted special customs privileges to the league together with the rights to build a guild house in the city of London, the Guildhalla Teutonicorum, and to appoint an alderman to represent their interests. The Hansa merchants were prevailed upon by Edward 1 to contribute 210 marks sterling to repair Bishopsgate, one of the gate houses to the City of London and to covenant that they and their successors would pay for its future repair. The gate was rebuilt in 1479 at the expense of the German merchants in London. At Kings Lynn the old Hansa factory still exists and has been fully restored.

It was in the face of this powerful opposition that the English textile industry was established.

The Available dyes and mordants

In researching the specific dyes and dyeing techniques of the medieval period one is relying heavily on Italian sources. The Italians were undoubtedly the leading dyers and textile producers of the period and are virtually our only contemporary source of information. Since the Italians dominated the market in Europe for high quality cloth, the quality of dyed cloth produced elsewhere in Europe must have been much inferior. Only the common indigenous dyestuffs would have been widely available elsewhere. Italian dyeing was not necessarily typical of the dye industry in Europe generally.

The following dyestuffs and mordants to which we have contemporary reference were traded in Italy in the 14th century, according to the archives of Francesco di Datini in Florence and Prato:-

Woad	Saffron	Red and white tartar
Kermes	Gum arabic	Orchil
Indigo	Orpiment	Roch alum
Brasilwood	Indian lac	Galls for tannin
Sandelwood	Madder	

Textiles – wool and woollen cloth of various qualities, silk, linen, cotton and brocades.

One of the few contemporary books we have on medieval dyeing is the Plictho written by Gioanventura Rossetti in 1548. The word Plictho means the collection and the sub title is the Instructions in the Art of the Dyers which Teaches the Dying *(sic)* of Woollen Cloths, Linens, Cottons and Silk by the Great Art as well as by the Common. In the Plictho we have a comprehensive list of dyes, mordants and dye recipes.

This gives a picture of late medieval Italian textile dyeing. From this there appear to be about 25 specific dyes giving various shades of red, yellow, blue, black and brown. These colours could be modified with about a dozen mordants including tannins, acids and alkalies. In addition of course these colours could be modified by dyeing with more than one dye. This would give greens, purples, orange, pink etc. Dyes would normally not be mixed but the cloth would be immersed in a series of vats. The final colours would also be modified by the amount of dye used and the length of time of immersion and the temperature and acidity of the vat. In practice this would increase enormously the range of hues and shades available to the dyer. Furthermore the type and condition of the fabric to be dyed would also affect the final colour.

In addition to those given above from the Datini archives, Rosetti lists the following additional dyes and mordants :-

Polish cochineal	Alkannet	Weld
Dyer's broom	Turmeric	Young fustic
Pomegranate	Sage	Sugar of lead
Fenugreek	Verdigris	Iron and iron salts
Persian berries	Black alder	
Walnut	Sumach	
Litharge	Bitter almonds	

It is difficult to gauge how many of the exotic dyestuffs reached England. Certainly imported indigo was not used by English dyers until the late 16th century and later still in France and Germany. Cotton was not commonly used in England until about 1750. Chaucer mentions madder, weld and woad in his short poem The Former Age

By modern standards the treatment of the subject of dyeing in the Plictho is very unsystematic. However the recipes can be followed and form the basis for researching late medieval methods of dyeing in Italy. The enormous demand throughout Europe for Italian cloth testifies to their quality compared with that available from other sources.

Black

Dyeing black has always presented special difficulties. Rossetti writing in 1548, and not being himself a dyer he was dependant on the information the dyers were prepared to give him. There are in the Plictho, some twenty separate recipes for black on wool, wool skeins, silk and leather. In principle the black produced by the "Great Art" was made by dyeing the cloth dark blue and deepening the colour with other dyes. For blacks made by the "Lesser Art" the principle ingredients on wool were, according to Rossetti, iron acetate, made by dissolving iron filings in vinegar and tannin from oak galls.

The problem with iron salts is their tendency to rot wool. The practice was to use the minimum amount of iron salts to "sadden " the cloth and then dye with tannin and any other dye such as red, blue or yellow to give a more solid colour which resulted in a blue/black, red/black or yellow/black. A jet black was difficult to produce before the introduction of logwood. One of Rossetti's recipes used annatto as a preliminary treatment. This produces a brown colour, and this dye is soluble in water with an alkali present. However in Rossetti's recipe wine was added with the annatto. This together with oak galls and iron sulphate gave a good black on woollen cloth.

The alternative was to mordant with blue from the woad vat. By the 17th Century with the introduction of logwood from Central America, it was mandatory for black cloth dyed with logwood in England and France to be first dyed with woad or indigo. The cloth would be carefully washed and rinsed after dyeing. A weak solution of gum Arabic was commonly used to stiffen or give body to the cloth.

The best tannin was obtained by boiling oak galls, which had been ground to a fine powder. Rossetti makes the point that dyeing high quality cloth required more care than for dyeing cheap cloth. To remove the smell of oil from wool it was recommended that the wool was washed in water in which cypress wood sawdust or hedge mustard had been boiled. This also avoided spots or staining due to the presence of oil.

Rossetti states that either rainwater or river water could be used for dyeing. This suggests that no regard was paid to the hardness or other minerals dissolved in the water. Their main concern was only that the water should be clean and the same kind of water used consistently.

Rossetti was writing before logwood had been discovered in Central America. Logwood (Haematoxylon campechianum) appears to have been the first natural dyestuff which produced a true jet black on textiles. There is a reference to the use of blue as a base for black in the

Elizabethan regulations for black dyeing.(See appendix 3). This Act of Parliament is confusing in several ways. Firstly the intention was to place a complete embargo on the use of logwood. The ostensible reason was that logwood was not considered a fast dye, but later acts repealing this state that the dyers had now found ways of using the logwood to give black. The real reason was probably to exclude a new imported dyestuff in the face of the dyers' conservatism and established practices. Eventually the best blacks on wool and silk were obtained with logwood. The Act also forbids the use of galls and madder except on blue cloth to produce black. The Act makes no mention of iron salts which were essential ingredients and used at that time for virtually all blacks. The reason for this omission was most probably simply that the act was not intended to instruct the public in black dyeing or to reveal the secrets of the dyers but simply to prohibit a practice that the professional dyers considered inimical to their interests.

In Rossetti's first recipe "To make black dyeings on yarn or linens" the ingredients are :-

Flour of rye made into a dough, but liquefied and kept warm. 10 litres.
Fine iron filings   75 lbs.
Hot water   6 buckets
Blackberry leaves equal in weight to the cloth to be dyed.

Alternative dye recipes for black:-
1) Oak galls in place of the blackberry leaves. Repeated immersion of the cloth in the dye vat was necessary to obtain a deep black colour.
2) Alder bark with an iron mordant, with a second dyeing with oak galls.

3) Walnut husks and juice of pomegranate fruit.
4) Eggshells boiled in water, iron filings, galls, alum, urine, and gum Arabic.
5) Litharge (lead oxide) and quicklime.
6) Burnt shells of peaches boiled with linseed oil.

Blue

The principle source of blue dye was indigo derived from woad. A blue colour could also be derived from Archil with lime as an alkali, or copper sulphate. Indigo from the East was available in Italy at least as early as 1400AD. As many as 18 different blues are listed. Watchet and Plunket were shades of blue. The word watchet, has been used to denote a colour from the 12th century onwards. Cloth was manufactured at Watchet in Somerset, but the connection with blue dye is unknown. Chaucer mentions watchet in The Miller's Tale –

Yclad he was ful smal and proprely
All in a kirtel of light waget (watchet)

The word is used by many other writers, including Shakespeare, Lyly, Campden, Collins and Lamb[9]. Small boats known as Watchet flatties were traditionally painted outside with watchett blue.

Mary Queen of Scots wore knitted stockings of watchett blue for her execution on 8th. Feb. 1586, and King Charles 1 wore a waistcoat of watchett blue for his execution on 30th. Jan. 1649. Hakluyt, in 1589 speaks of "Mariners attired in watchet or skie-coloured clothe".

The importance of woad as the source of blue indigo dye is indicated in John Stow's, A survey of London 1598, quoting William Fitzstephen's description of London in 1170:-

"No woad was stowed or harboured in this city (of London), but all was presently sold in the ships, except by licence purchased of the sheriffs, till of more later time; to wit, in the year 1236 Andrew Bokerell, being mayor, by assent of the principal citizens, the merchants of Amiens, Nele and Corby, purchased letters insealed with the common seal of this city. that they when they come might harbour their woads, and therefore should give the mayor every year fifty marks sterling; and the same year they give one hundred pounds towards the conveying of water from Tybourn to the city. Also the merchants of Normandy made fine for licence to harbour their woads till it was otherwise provided in the year 1263, Thomas Fitz Thomas being mayor, etc. which proveth that then as afore, they were here amongst other nations privileged."

The colours resulting from so-called natural dyes that are seen in textiles in museums were not simply found in Nature, but were won by a series of technologies from their natural raw material sources. The use of indigo, whatever its source is a special case because the plants from which it was obtained do not actually contain indigo and it was made during the processing.. Indigo is indeed an artefact. Rossetti refers to all the following colours for dyed cloth in the Plictho of 1548:-

Bark shade   from alum, kermes, madder, lime, brazilwood, young fustic

PLATE 1

Logwood dyed on blue to give
a permanent black on wool

PLATE 2

Medieval lead seals
By courtesy of the Museum of London

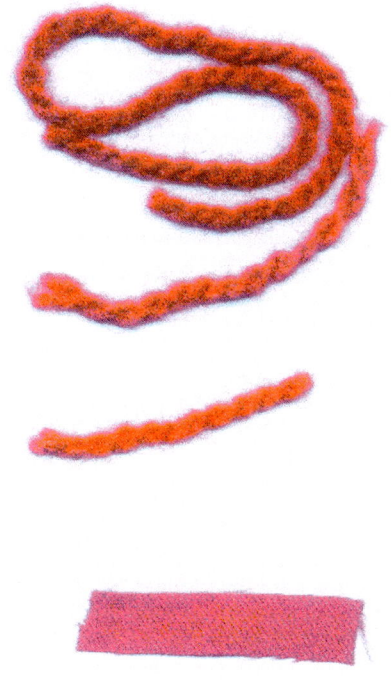

PLATE 3

Wool dyed with the Kermes beetle
by Dr Dominique Cardon

PLATE 4

Reds available before 1600

PLATE 5

Yellow from weld and green from weld and woad

PLATE 6

The Woad plant in its first year

PLATE 7

The Weld plant or Dyers Rocket

PLATE 8

The medieval Wool House once used as an alum warehouse.

Black	from burnt peach stones and linseed oil
Brown/Camel	from oak galls and iron sulphate Plate
Cardinal shade	from alum, kermes, madder, brazilwood, lime and tartar
Faded blood	from alum, madder, brazilwood, tartar
Green	from copper sulphate, vinegar, sal ammoniac, alum, salt, copper filings
Grey	from oak galls and iron sulphate
Half scarlet	on wool from bran and chaff, alum, tartar, madder, lime and oxblood. This recipe appears to be an early attempt to produce Turkey Red.
Madder red	from alum and madder
Morello	from alum, kermes, madder, brazilwood,
Orange	from alum, kermes, madder, brazil, young fustic
Peacock blue	from alum, kermes, madder, brazilwood and lime
Pheasant blue	from alum, tartar, madder, brazilwood and lime
Pink	
Quince	from alum, kermes, weld, young fustic
Red	
Rose Cardinal	
Rusty red	from white vinegar, rusty iron, alum, weld and ammonia
Scarlet	from kermes, alum, tartaric acid and bran
Tawney	from alum, young fustic and iron sulphate

Yellow from white of eggs, fig wood, salt and saffron

One difficulty occurs in dyeing with a pure woad vat; the amount of indigo in the processed woad is rather limited and could not in medieval times be increased with the addition of imported tropical indigo. The result is that it is very difficult to get the dye to penetrate woven woollen cloth. It seems very probable that the dyers would dye the wool or yarn before it was woven into cloth. When pure indigo became available and could be added to the woad vat this difficulty was overcome.

A number of medieval recipes require the use of lead, mercury or arsenic as mordants, in the form of soluble salts. These however are too poisonous to be used in dye recipes today and have therefore been excluded from this review.

Painted Cloth

Painted cloth was a very common alternative to dyed cloth on linen or silk and for this reason it is included. The cloth was stretched on a frame and sized with "gesso sottile" or plaster of Paris mixed with starch and sugar. The drawing or pattern was sketched on the cloth with charcoal. Either pigment or dye mixed with gum arabic can then be painted on the cloth.

Standard methods of medieval dyeing

Recipes exist in the Plictho for dyeing of:-
wool
cotton

silk
linen
thread or yarn
fustians
homespuns
woollen cloth and caps
velvets
satins
damasks
tabbies
nettings
taffetas
tannin leathers, feathers
horse hair
skins
furs
Parchment paper

The use of mordants and the affect of various acids and alkalis on colour were well understood. The sources from which the various dyestuffs and mordants were obtained were very important and provided some guarantee of consistent quality. The dyers needed a constant supply of known quality to allow them to produce matching colours from different batches of materials. Armenian Kermes or grain was considered superior to Spanish or Asian Kermes. Toulouse woad was considered the best on the London market and commanded a correspondingly higher price. Flanders madder was the best available. Different methods of production existed in different places and affected its value. By long experience the dyers came to recognise the varying qualities, and experienced factors or agents were employed to act as inspectors and buyers for the dyers.

Fabrics were rinsed carefully to remove soap before soaking the cloth in an alum mordant; otherwise a sticky alum soap would be deposited on the cloth. Wool was washed on the sheeps' back and then the fleeces were scoured or washed using stale urine (that is ammonia) to convert the lanolin in the wool to soap. The action of the urine would also improve the handle or softness of the wool. The wool could either be dyed in the wool, that is dyed before spinning, dyed as yarn or for the woven cloth to be dyed as a piece. Generally the best cloth was spun and woven from wool that had been dyed before spinning. The effect was that any unevenness in the dyeing could be removed in the process of carding, spinning and weaving.

The finishing of woollen cloth had reached a high state of perfection in Italy and particularly in Florence. English fleeces, particularly from the Cotswold were in great demand in Flanders and Italy. The reason for this is not clear since sheep were kept all over Europe and the wool varied with the breeds. A possible reason was that the mild damp Atlantic climate in Britain favoured the growth of grasslands through most of the year which allowed sheep to thrive without the stress of summer droughts This would ensure a consistent quality of the fleeces. Throughout the early Middle Ages wool fleeces were the principle export from Britain until eventually a cloth manufacturing industry was established. In 1350-60 an average of 32,000 sacks of wool was exported each year, and English wool commanded the highest prices in Italy. It is an interesting coincidence that it was only after 1600 when the new dyestuffs became available from Central America and Indigo from India and elsewhere that the change from English wool to Merino wool originating from Spain, took place.

Dyer's Alkanet

Alkanet (Alkanna tinctoria) is a member of the borage family. The chopped root of alkanet was used in dyeing.

There is only one recipe in the Plictho using alkanet as a dye:-
171 To dye hairs of dogs, of horses, and any other thing.

First take some clear water and wash very well in that place where you want to dye. When this is done, take some powder of the grass known as alkanet and let it stay to soak in enough water that it be covered, and let it stand for one night. Take the said powder, and wet it and put it where you want to dye thus washed. Paste up very well and then cover with a cloth of linen, and let it dry well, and then wash it and it is done.

Archil or Orchil

A red/purple dye was obtained from this lichen;a colour very similar to the molluscal imperial purple; it was frequently used as a substitute for this very expensive dye. This lichen (Roccella tinctoria) has been given various names. Lichen rocella by Linnaeus, archil, orchil, orchal, orchilla, archilla, tournsole, orseille and litmus. In the Plictho it is called horizello, orizello, tornexel or raspa. This lichen has been used with urine or ammonia throughout history. At various times the secret has been lost only to be revived later. Its chequered history has probably been due to over exploitation and its recovery due to new localities where it has been found in abundance. The history of murex purple and orchil lichen seem to be entertwined. After the collapse of the Roman empire there is very little reference to orchil until 1300AD. A Florentine merchant Federigo, whose family took the name Ruccelli after the dye, reintroduce it. By 1400 it is recorded in Marco Datini's papers that he was importing the lichen from Majorca. A descendant of the Ruccelli family published a manuscript in 1881 stating:

"Our ancestors were lichen dyers, and in that period there was no one in Florence nor even in all Italy except those ancestors of ours who knew how to dye with lichens. (One of them, after travelling in the Levant where the skills of lichen dyeing were still known, brought the secret back with him.) And this was the cause that gave so much wealth and good living to our family... and from this art of the lichen dye is derived the name of Rucellai."

Archil was frequently used as a top dye to other colours on silk. A dyer's manual from near Venice dating to the second half of the 15th century by Giovanni Rebora, devotes four chapters to the preparation and use of orchil and gives many recipes. He states "To recognise good raspe (orchil) look for the ones that are nicely coloured and tend towards purple.. Note that the orizela which has gone through (the fermentation process) must be used quickly – for those who keep it too long, it will go bad, and they will lose both the capital and the profit." The lichen was obtained from sources throughout Europe and the Middle East. The lichen was eventually discovered in the Canary Islands in the late 14th century. Orchil is mentioned in a statute of Henry V111 in 1533 and in Shakespeare's Richard 11 and Richard 111.

There are a number of recipes and references to archil or turnsole in the Plictho :-

43 To make blue

Measure archil or violet that is named turnsole and is good and perfect. When it is purchased ask for archil or violet. Put it in an apparatus according to the quantity and mix with live lime. If it is too thick put in some human urine and then mix well and make sure it is well mixed. The more the urine is old, the better.

82. To make archil.

Measure one hundred pounds scrapings of archil and then take 10 pounds alum of "catinum" pestled and fine and then put it in with the scrapings into a utensil. Incorporate together with human urine and knead these things with the hands as when one makes bread and pull it to one side of the trough or the box. With a trowel go spreading and working and then gather this mixture together in one corner and let it stand thus for four days. When it begins to show colour, mix it and return it to the corner.

Note, as it begins to get warm, mix it up four times a day and when it has become cool mix it two times a day and within twenty days, twice a week and smooth it with a brush dipped in wine according to what you see it needs.

Note, that as the said archil readily makes hands red, one must throw in so much wine that it be pasted well to advantage, so that it becomes thick in the manner of mud. With the trowel keep stirring and incorporating to advantage, until the end of 50 days, mixing the archil two or three times a day. In this time it will have become thick so that it will be good to use.

A Venetian dye recipe book of the late 17th century, the New Plico by Gallipidio Tallier, contains a recipe for a dark brown which uses orchil. According to E. Bancroft:-

The Italians... engrossed for a century (i.e early 1300s to early 1400s) all (the orchil) that could be procured...among the islands of the (Greek) Archipelago, and on the shores of the Mediterranean; until the discovery of the Canary Islands in 1402, by John de Bethencourt, a Norman, relieved the other nations of Europe from their dependence upon Italy for this commodity.

Eventually the expensive archil was replaced by cudbear(b) (Lecanora tartarea) by Cuthbert Gordon in the 19th century. This was a lichen found in Scotland. This in turn was replaced by Perkin's synthetic dye mauveine in 1860.

Brazilwood

Brazilwood from the Caesalpina sappan tree was imported from the East Indies. Only after the discovery of America was brasilwood brought in from the New World. It was used in Italy before this date, presumably brought in from the East. It was used in combination with alum mordant, tannin and gum arabic to give weight and stiffness to the fabric.

Fenugreek (Trigonella foenum graecum) Greek Hay

Fenugreek or Greek Hay is mentioned in the Plictho In combination with madder, bran, galls, vinegar and cinnabar.The purpose of the Fenugreek in this recipe is not clear.

Genista tinctoria or Dyer's Broom

There seems to be some confusion between Genista tinctoria and Spartium junceum or Spanish broom. Genista is native to northern Britain while Spanish broom is a Mediterranean plant. Most books on dyeing suggest that only the flower petals were used in dyeing. As a medieval dye this seems unlikely when in fact the whole plant will yield the yellow dye. The Plictho refers to "a half bundle of herba corniola (genista)" this does not seem to mean only the flower petals.

Indigo

Indigo was known to the Ancient Romans as a pigment obtained from India or Thailand. Hurry (p54) refers to woad being imported in Saxon times and again in the 12th century. The history of woad is covered by the first book in this series – The History of Woad and the Medieval Woad Vat.

Imperial Purple

Imperial purple, otherwise known as Tyrian purple. Murex purple or dibromo-indigotin is thought of mainly as a classical dye. It was in fact produced commercially in Constantinople until the sack of that city in 1453. It does therefore qualify also as a medieval dye. The details of its use as a commercial dyestuff are covered in some detail in the booklet – Imperial or Tyrian Purple – already published in this series.

Kermes or Grain and Polish Cochineal

Kermes and Polish Cochineal were the European equivalent to the Cochineal imported from Central America by the Spanish during the 16th century.

Rossetti was evidently under the impression that the kermes beetles, known as grain, were berries. Certainly the kermes on the kermes oaks could be easily mistaken for berries. Rossetti states that the best came from Armenia, Asia and Spain in that order. In fact the beetle and the Kermes oak can be found around most of the Mediterranean Sea, including southern France. Kermes was replaced by cochineal, originally from Mexico which produces much more of the dye. Before the introduction of tin chloride as a mordant in 1607 crimsons and scarlets were made by mordanting the cloth with starch from flour or bran and alum, acidified water and cream of tartar. Tannin from galls was also used for certain shades of crimson. The yellowish or flame coloured scarlets became very popular much later. The older kermes scarlets prepared without tin chloride became known as French or Venetian scarlets. These according to Bemiss were less lustrous and browner than the cochineal and tin scarlets.

Cochineal replaced kermes in the 1600 century after its introduction from central America by the Spanish. The cochineal was reputed to contain four times as much dye as Kermes[8]

Madder

Madder was used as a dye since prehistoric times for reds and browns, but was not on its own suitable for the expensive crimsons and scarlets. There were colours known as half, or bastard scarlets which were produced by combining madder with kermes. A scarlet could be obtained using madder on alumed wool with the water made alkaline. The cloth would be dyed in the wool to ensure the maximum take up of the dye and intensity of colour. Madder could be obtained in various qualities depending on its place of origin and the process of sorting, drying and preparation. It could also be ground into a powder. Madder was grown near Rome in the first century AD. according to Pliny the Elder. There are several species of madder which all produce the red alizarin in varying quantities. A yellow as well as a red dye exists in madder. If the dyestuff is boiled then a yellow dye is also released which results in an orange colour or various shades of brown. Madder requires alum as a mordant to produce a fast colour.

1. madder with alum added to the dye liquor gives a bright orange with acidic water
2. madder with wool gives a bright brick red, if the water is alkaline.
3. Madder boiled gives brown shades.

Persian Berries

Persian berries (Rhamnus tinctorius et al.) were used in Europe for dyeing in the medieval period, for various shades of yellow but their use was much less common in the 18th century dyers except by French silk dyers. . Hats and other garments worn by Jews were dyed with Persian berries. The red unripe berries were used in dyeing. Persian berries were known as the "grain of Avignon" but were produced in other places in Europe.[5]

Pomegranate

The peel of the fruit, the stems and the roots of the pomegranate were used in dyeing in medieval Italy. With alum or iron salts, it would give yellow or black respectively. In the Plictho there are two recipes for making black using pomegranates. In addition the hulls of fresh walnuts, iron filings, alum and brazilwood.

Saffron

Saffron (Crocus sativa) must not be confused with the autumn crocus (Colchicum autumnale). The saffron crocus has three stamens, while the autumn crocus has six stamens, and the leaves of the autumn crocus do not appear until the Spring. The saffron crocus is a member of the Iris family. Saffron when collected in bulk was known as saffron hay. It has been estimated that one ounce of saffron contains about 12,500 stamens and an acre of saffron would yield as much as 20 pounds of dried saffron.

The word saffron is derived from the Arabic za'faran and is mentioned in the Bible and by Pliny the Elder. Saffron was grown extensively in the Middle Ages, and in England particularly around Saffron Walden. The plants are perennial and were normally lifted every three years. The flowers with their stigmas were harvested in the autumn in late October to early November. The stigmas were then carefully separated from the petals, dried and used as a dyestuff, food colourant and as an ingredient in medicines. Saffron was grown at Saffron Walden up to the end of the

18th. Century. Saffron must always have been incredibly expensive and have resulted in very expensive dyed cloth.. If used at all it would be for small items of decorative clothing or head gear.

Saffron stigmas are also superficially very similar to the dried flowers of the safflower plant (Carthamus tinctoria), which was also used for textile dyeing. Safflower is sometimes sold to tourists under the name Safran as if it were saffron. The price alone should indicate the confusion. On close inspection the saffron consists of individual stigma with a deep red broader end and a thin tail about 2 centimetres long tipped with yellow. The safflower consists of red florets sometimes still in one piece about 1 centimetre long with the centre of the floret tipped yellow.

Both saffron and safflower were used as dyes since ancient Egyptian times. Safflower is now naturalised in Europe. Saffron has been cultivated so long that the plant is sterile and is not found in the wild state. Surprisingly safflower does not appear to have been used by professional dyers in the middle ages but is included as a dyestuff in 18th century manuals; while saffron was a common dyestuff before 1600 but seems to be redundant after this date. Saffron was also used in 15th century Florence, mixed with indigo to give a green pigment called "verde azurro" . Saffron was also used at the same time to dye linen and to make a green pigment with verdigris (copper sulphate) and vinegar.

Sticklac

Sticklac was a dyestuff imported from the East. It is referred in the Plictho in the 16th century and was still in use as a dyestuff into the 19th century. Lac is a waxy secretion from an insect named Laccifer lacca and is found in India, Indochina, the Philippines and Sri Lanka, and exists on fig, banyan and other trees. Shellac is also made from Sticklac. As a dye it provided a cheaper source of red than cochineal or kermes. The red dye must be separated from the resin before use.

Tannins

Tannin was both a mordant for a range of colours and an essential ingredient for black and brown. The tannin could be derived from a wide range of galls, plant material, particularly oak bark and blackberry leaves.

Oak galls

The tannin was extracted from oak galls by grinding them to a powder and boiling in a vat. It was also used in black ink with iron salts and gum Arabic. William Shakespeare, in Twelfth Night remarks "Let there be gall enough in thy ink." Galls can occur on a wide variety of plants but the oak apple galls are the ones normally associated with dyeing. They are formed as a result of insect attack and are an abnormal growth of plant cells. Inside, the insect egg or larvae is surrounded by a protein rich nutritive tissue[7]. This in turn is surrounded by a thick wall rich in lignin and tannin.

Other sources of tannin include Sumaces and walnut hulls.

Sage

Sage (Salvia officinalis) is one of the more obscure dyestuffs referred to in the Plictho. It was used with vinegar and saffron for yellow, with cinnabar for red and verdigris for green.

Weld

Weld or Dyer's Rocket (Reseda luteola) is a very ancient dyestuff and has been a principle source of yellow dye since Roman times. This plant is easily grown and can be dried like hay. It is also available from Holland finely ground as a powder. Madder, weld and woad are mentioned by Geoffrey Chaucer as the three principle dyestuffs in use in 14th century England.

Woad

The history of woad is covered more extensively in book No.1 of this series. Woad was used for indigo dyeing in Ancient Egypt (Cardon) and in Ancient Greece (Brunello) but the indigo dye was obtained from the fresh leaves fermented in stale urine. This process is slow but extracts the indigo, or its precursor from the leaves and dissolves the indigo to its leuco form ready for dyeing the cloth. By the Middle Ages and probably very much earlier, the method used in Europe was to preserve the woad and form the indigo in woad balls and allow it to dry. These were subsequently crushed, fermented again, or couched and finally fermented in an alkaline vat.

The woad industry in the fenlands originated only after the fenlands were drained in the 17th century. There the industry continued until 1930 on a very small scale.

At Reading University the contents of a woad have been analysed. This has resulted in a number of published academic papers[10].

Young fustic

Young Fustic or Venetian Sumac (Cotinus coggygria) is a common shrub in Mediterranean countries. The heart-wood of the tree is deep yellow in colour and is used as the dyestuff. This was used throughout the medieval period as a source of a deep golden yellow. The tree is now commonly grown as an ornamental garden plant, known as the wig or smoke tree.

Mordant used in 1548 Italy in: -

The Use of Acids and Alkalis

Brunello states in his Art of Dyeing in the History of Mankind (P260) that the preparation of sulphuric acid by the burning of sulphur with saltpetre was mentioned as early as the Middle Ages by Albertus Magnus (1193-1280) and also by Basilio Valentino (1450). In the $14t^h$ century Pseudo-Geber prepared it by distilling alum with iron sulphate. In 1613 Angelo Sala from Vicenza described a method of obtaining sulphuric acid by burning sulphur in very moist air. This method was then modified by LaFévre and Lemery in 1660. Only in 1740 however was the first industrial plant built in England near London, the work of Ward and Richmond, who burned sulphur and saltpetre in an iron capsule and then condensed the steam with balls of glass. Large scale production in lead chambers began in 1746 at Birmingham (Roebuck and Garbett). This led to the manufacture of chlorine from black oxide of manganese, sea salt and sulphuric acid in 1785 in France and made possible the manufacture of bleach.

Verdigris

Copper sulphate can be used in place of verdigris. Verdigris itself is a naturally occurring green patina of basic salts of copper. Its composition varies depending on the atmospheric conditions. It includes the basic carbonate, sulphate and sometimes the chloride of copper. The Plictho includes some ten recipes using verdigris. These are mainly for green dyes when combined with weld or other yellow dyestuffs.

Iron salts

Iron in the form of a soluble salt was a common mordant particularly for black This was often combined with various tannins. The iron salts could be easily obtained by placing iron filings in vinegar. Iron however tends to rot wool and was therefore used sparingly. One technique was to dye the wool to a deep blue with indigo or woad and then top dye using tannin and iron salts. Dark blue could be made black using other dyes for top dyeing to give a blue/black or red/black. A jet black was difficult to obtain before the use of logwood. Copperas or green vitriol were other names for iron sulphate.

Wood ash

Ash was obtained from wood fires, particularly oak and refined by filtering like flour to remove charcoal. This gave a fine white powder, which was largely potassium carbonate known as potash. This was used to create alkaline solutions for dyebaths. The ash usually settles to the bottom without affecting the dyed fabric. It was also used in preparing skins for tannin.

Urine

Stale Urine was commonly used in dyeing and in other industrial processes until the manufacture of ammonia from coal tar residues in the 19th century. In every case where urine is mentioned standard household ammonia can be substituted.

Saltpetre

There is one recipe in the Plictho where saltpetre is used to produce a green dye. The saltpetre was used with vinegar, sal ammoniac and a "little common lye" which presumably was stale urine. This was then used on light blue cloth to give green

Alum

Alum or potash alum is aluminium potassium sulphate, which occurs naturally as the mineral kalinite. It is very soluble in hot water and was used as a mordant in dyeing with natural dyes from the very earliest periods. Alum in Viking times apparently was extracted from stag moss (Lycopodium complanatum). Alum in the Middle Ages was a monopoly of the Italians and was obtained from mines in Turkey. Later the mineral was found in Italy itself. By the 17th century alum was derived from deposits in Yorkshire. Alum was also used in tannin and in finishing leather goods for white leather.

Pearl Ash

Pearl ash or potash is potassium carbonate and is used in dyeing and wool finishing, and as an alkali. It was obtained from wood ash. Pearl ash should not be confused with cream of tartar which is potassium hydrogentartrate or tartaric acid (argol). This was obtained originally from deposits in wine barrels..

Bran

Bran was an ingredient that was used with a number of dyestuffs. It appears to have been used in woad vats to encourage fermentation and to give weight or "body" to fabrics.Bran was used in the finishing of black fabrics.

Conclusions

In the medieval period Europe saw an immense advance in the art of dyeing and finishing of cloth. The growth in the textile trade accompanied a growth in population. However as Professor Brunello observes in The Art of Dyeing in the History of Mankind, apart from the notable exception of fabric printing there was virtually no change in the equipment of dye houses throughout this period. Indeed an 18th century dyer would have been at home in a dye house in classical Pompei.. Only with the advances of the industrial revolution and the use of water, steam and electrical power was the textile trade transformed. Not only were the processes mechanised, but finally the introduction of the new synthetic dyes changed textile dyeing from a craft to a science based on complex chemistry.

APPENDICES

1) 15th. century recipe for the woad vat

A Recipe for dyeing with woad from the Archives of the Guild of l'Arte della Lana, Florence in 1418 translated by Dr Dominique Cardon
Ref. Arte Lana della, Biblioteca Riccardiana, Florence, Codex 2580, fo.141vo-147, February 1418,.

Here after I shall write the order and way of dyeing with woad, which is usually done by the body of Dyers of Florence, and is called l'Arte minore, or dyeing in woad.
1) Perse Blues, (Darkest blue)
    (first primed in old blue vats, then finished in new vat [corredo or prime] with up to 5 dips)
2) The azzurini (corredo vat)
    azure blues,
    sky blues for Rome(these are darker),
    sky blues according to our fashions,
3) Sbiadati blues
    dark sbiadati blues
    light sbiadati blues,
4) Turkish blues
Turkish blues in two dippings. Turkish blues which are in between these and the darkened ones,
Darkened Turkish blues.
Turkish blues obtained straight away, which are lighter than the darkened ones and Turkish blues lighter than the above mentioned,
5) Allazzati blues
    strong allazzati
    light allazatti

lighter allazatti (the lightest blue specified)

All these colours are obtained by way of the working of the vat that I will describe here after. And in summertime, it is usually set around the 22nd hour of the day, and in winter, another timetable is used, as you will see.
Beginning in the month of February 1418

The woad vat is set according to the manner of Florence, usually with 400 lbs. about the 16th. hour of the day, putting the said plant, that is woad, into the vat used for this, and let's say that the amount of clear water which is put for the aforesaid quantity of woad be around 20 barrels. And you must know that in all things that has to be done, you must pay attention to the quality of the woad, whether it is of great or little strength, and in all things, use one's sight, which experience will help you to understand. The said water must be poured into the said vat when it boils and is boiling, and the footing is given with 80 lbs. of oak ash that looks white; and the said ash should be fresh, not older than 4 to 6 months, because the fresher it is, the stronger.. And then one must lift the bath very thoroughly with the rakes, together with the woad and with the aforesaid ash, and then it will make the copper scales, that is a greenish scum.

One must let it stand all day until the next morning at the 9th. hour, which leads to the next day. And it might happen that such woad would, for the footing, might need 10 lbs. more of the aforesaid oak ash; and the said vat from the beginning, and then all the while it is not being worked, should be kept covered with the wooden lid, a mule blanket, not so much to prevent the exhalation of fumes, but in order to keep the aforesaid woadvat warm.

And at the 9th. hour, one must take off the covers of the said vat and pestle it with great energy, that is pounding it well and stirring it well, using the sticks; and when it is on the verge of being ripe, it will make the copper scales, that is, you will see the scum collect itself on the surface, a bluish scum like violet comes up, and then you can see that the colour has started to come.

Then, after letting it stand for 3 hours or so, one uncovers the said vat again, nearly at the 12th. hour and looks at the said vat. But when the colour does not arrive and come soon, usually one gives it 1 mina of bran, just plain, and put it into the bath. But if you see that you can do without the bran, don't put any, because it is a bad solution and not to be resorted to willingly.

But when you have examined the said vat at the aforesaid hour and you push into the bath with the rake, then with your eyes and nose, you must see whether it needs ash, lifting up the plant. The sign for the nose is that it should give out a comforting smell, like that of something mature; and then if you turn over the said plant in the said vat, you'll see something like a pen stroke of a greenish tinge, like the colour of a "gone off" sauce; and from these two signs, that is the one from the nose and that from the eyes, and when you see that there is this greenish tinge, you put 25 lbs. of oak-ash into it - which is like giving it to eat. And these ashes, you put them in when the vat is hungry; they must be softer, or rather of less strength than the ashes you have put at the beginning of the bath, i.e., this ash must be more than 6 months old so that it gets staler and of less substance, that way it is good. This now, is to comfort the vat, for if one did not comfort it, the colour would vanish into fumes. And this is called the first stirring. And when you give it this ash, you must put in 2 bigonciuoli of boiling water into it, to keep it warm; and moreover, cover it down before letting it stand, as has been said above.

And then, about three hours later, nearly at the 15th. hour, that is, at the hour of tierce, you take the covers off and examine the said vat, and then you must see, from the aforesaid signs, whether it needs ash. If not, wait a little and when you see the said signs, give it 25lbs. more of the said softer ash, as explained before, giving it also 2 or 3 barrels of boiling water. And to comfort the vat, it would be even better, instead of the said water, to give it some boiling madder dye-bath, as has been said before, i.e. the bath for dyeing woollen cloth into imitation scarlet. It is of great comfort to the said vat, and to be given when needed. For the woad vat is like a man, that wants to eat and drink, otherwise he dies; and so does the colour in the vat, that would vanish into fumes if it was not refreshed when it needs it. And then one must let it stand, and this aforesaid stirring is called the 2nd. stirring.

When it has stood 3 hours, which leads approximately to the hour of none, you must examine whether it needs ashes or anything else, from the same signs, and if you see that it does, give it 25 lbs. more of ash and 2 or 3 bigonciuoli of boiling water or boiling madder dye-bath, or as you deem wise. And you must know that a connoisseur would know from far away, by his nose, if the colour was on the verge of going off. The sign, for the eye, would be if you happened to see the bath becoming yellow, like gold; then it needs to be rescued with the things afore described. And if it doesn't need them, let it stand well covered. And then at vespers, take the covers off and mind again the said signs, and if needed, give it again 25 lbs. of ashes with 2 or 3 buckets of boiling water to warm up the bath, as was said before. And this is called the 3rd. stirring, when you will give all these things in the same way.

And then the vat is ready to work. And one must fill up the vat to the top with boiling water and cover it down with the wooden lid and a donkey blanket, as said before, in order to keep the said bath warm.

And then in the evening at the 3rd hour, set it to work, putting in a piece of cloth or a wet of wool with the net.

And during the first dip, one can do 9 or 10 turns, either of cloth-pieces or of wool-wets with the net and during these turns, the bath gets lower.

Then it must be stir very well, lifting the liquid, the ash and the plant of the said woad and giving it 8 or 10 buckets of clear water, and then cover it down. And from then on, one can dye every 2 hours or so.

And then you must stir again with the sticks and go on dyeing as long as one can see there is some colour substance left.

The cloths dyed in dark shades of woad are dyed first, when the vat is in corredo, which corredo is called "prime", before these shades are dyed, and after that, when there is little colour left, one dyes into Turkish or allazatti blues.

Notice that if you want to dye with woad in small quantities, in a small vat, you must then keep it warm with sawdust. Note also that burnt juniper, like big lumps of coal, covered with the same juniper ash, keeps burning under this ash - according to what is said - for a whole year at least - whatever the truth there may be in that, I'm not sure.

Notice that the perse blues are primed in many baths used for wool and cloth, then finished in corredo, like the azzurini. Be informed, that ashes are added depending on the type of woad, either at the 1st, 2nd., or 3rd or 4th. or 5th. dip, according to whether it's needed.

The madder dye bath doesn't need to be given warm rather than cold, then it is put to the comfort of the bath when it needs it; to have some near at hand, very often, it is kept in a small vat during 10 to 12 days.

Here after I'll write a text obtained from N. do Vino, woad-coucher, and he used to express himself in the following way. "Indeed it is true what is written on the art of dyeing with woad, that it is deemed a manner of alchemy and that it cannot be properly described, nor even explained, but that if one wants to understand it, one must attend the thing. For I could describe to you the names of the things, but you won't understand the smells nor the timing of it because they cannot be described. I can give you an image of the way in which I can describe it to you. Let us suppose that a surgeon should want me to understand how he had cured a sick man or intended to cure him and said to me - who is ill informed or ignorant in this: "I got him rid of the hectic fever with lectuaries and hyssop"; I should know that he would have cured him with these things, but I should not know either at what times he had given them to him, nor in what manner, nor should I know this disease or these medicines. Thus you must realise that what I can write for you about this matter only is the names of the thing but not the ways, because we judge about everything with the smell and our nose; and this is our foundation.

In order for you to learn the ways we know to get colour out of woad: we have a certain vat, holding 6 cognia or so, and we take 400 lbs. of woad and 90 or 100 lbs. of ash, according to its strength - the strongest possible. And we put everything together in the vat, and we have hot water simmering and we put enough of it to fill up the vat to the 4/5. And when we set the vat - let us say on a Monday, at the 17th. hour, or the 18th. or the 19th. then on the following Tuesday, at the 11th. hour we pestle it down with some sticks, but without taking it out of the vat. (Very often by that time, it has started giving colour, but often also it hasn't; most of the time the colour comes out during this pestling and stirring that is done.) Now I must see to the smell, whether it is domestic or wild - these are the words which are used - and the smell is dry if it doesn't make a blue foam when I stir the vat. In this case I make it move on with bran and madder water, or I just wait, according to whether I think there is time.

And when the woad has given some blue, I wait until it gets the sweet smell and when it starts giving colour, I give it one measure of ash of 3/4 of staio or more. And most of the time, this takes place around the 14th. hour.

If I have fed it well, I feed it again another time, at the 16th. hour.

If at the second stirring it requires it, at the 18th. hour we will give it another time the same measure of ash, not as strong a kind as the previous one.

Then I re-examine it at the 21st. hour and if it needs more ash, I give it some. At all these stirrings, it must have the sweet smell, that is, domestic.

Then I fill it up with hot water and I don't touch it before the evening, i.e. at the time of the Ave Maria. and I mind whether it needs ash or bran, and I give some of it.

Then I start working it, from 2 to 6, and then I re-examine it. If I find it ripe, that is sweet smelling, I give it some ash, according to what it needs. If the vat has started to give the colour in good time, it needs 2/3 the ash measure to stay in good condition. And then it is worked continuously until 13, and after that, whenever it wants to, it goes on working until the evening.

And then it is given 2/3 of the said ash-measure and left to stand until the next morning.

And then it is worked all day long, adding ash in the evening; and it goes on working the next day. And that is the way of a vat that works well.

Again I want to give you another instance of the woad vat; that is, the vat is likened to the nature of man, who is born and wants to eat from time to time as he needs it, and when he should be put to his nurse's breast. For if he was given so much to eat that he could not digest it, it would make him sick, just as, if he was not given enough, nature would not have its count and he would die. So does it happen with a vat that is fed too much, that is which gets the ash too soon, when the smell is not sweet yet, and so it gets sick and becomes hypertrophic and on the other hand, if it does not get it in time, it starves and loses the colour. So that it would only be possible to understand all this too one who would keep a good eye to certain signs and also, indeed the smell and the nose the smell being the most important thing, as said before.

2) Ordinance of the Bristol Guild of Dyers in 1439

From the Little Red Book of Bristol

To the worshipful and reverent Sirs the Mayor Sherriff Bailiffs and all the worthy men of the Common Counsel of the town of Bristol beseech meekly your humble Co- burgesses all the masters of the craft cleped Dyers of the town of Bristol that their worshipful Sirs as the said beseechers hath divers ordnances granted unto them long time past by your worthy predecessors, which ordinances beth enrolled in the red paper of the Guildhall and for as much as dyers trepassers of them dreadeth not to contrary and trespass against the ordinances aforesaid nor of the pains and amercements of it because more warrant wherethough that the said craft is greatly hindered and slandered please it to your most sad discretions for to oversee the said ordinances all and singular them to approve ratify and confirm in writing under your common seal as well as for the commonalty of the said town as for the better governance of the said craft and then to put into due execution reserving unto you and all your successors plain power and authority at all times to repeal undo make less and increase the same ordinances to your pleasure as well as for the profit and wealth of the said commune as of the said craft the tenor of which followeth in these words

In the first it was ordained and assented that two masters of the said craft everywhere be chosen by common assent of all the masters of the said craft in the said town of Bristol and their names be presented to the mayor in full court of the Guildhall and there be sworn upon the book within the quinzaine of St. Michael at the furthest, well and truly to survey all manner defaults which from that time forward shall be do in cloth dyed as in wool put in woad within the franchise of Bristow and if any damage or default be do in any person in default of dyeing be any man or woman of the same craft that then he shall pay sufficient amends to the party endamaged after the discretion of the foresaid masters, and of four other indifferent persons chosen by the mayor and his council them as the trepass shall axe, and if it be so that any man or woman will not stand to the ordinances and the award of the two masters another 4 indifferent persons chosen by the mayor as it is aforesaid that then the mayor and his council that shall be for the time, shall compel him to do, pay and make gree to the person so endangered all that shall be adjudged and decreed, and in case that the said two masters after such other made be negligent in doing their office touching the said craft that then they shall be punished and amerced after the advice of the mayor and of the court aforesaid to the use of the chamber and to the commune profit of the said craft then that no servant nor apprentice for this time forward be accepted to the liberties of Bristow to be burgesses sworn to occupy the said craft unto it be witnessed to the court to fore the mayor of Bristow by the said two masters that he is able and well learned in the craft of dyers for to swaftly ward and keep good all people which use to be served for their money in the occupation of the craft aforesaid and if any master of the said craft make any such servant or apprentice burgess but he be able and well learned in the aforesaid craft as it is above said he shall renne on the pain at everytime 20s. That is to say to the work of the commune and to the light of the said craft, without any pardon saving at all times that the mayor of Bristow have jurisdiction and power to accept and make burgess of every person presented as it hath been used and accustomed afore this time, this ordinance not with standing

(To this is appended the note in Latin – John Shopward was mayor in 1445.)

Item for as much as many times afore this time dyvers people which hath not be apprentices, servants nor masters of the same craft, as other people which beth of other crafts not knowing nor konning in the aforesaid craft of dyers hath taken upon them to dye certain clothes and wool put in woad as well of the good folk of the said town as of the country about which same cloth because of evil governance and in default of konning of such folk both greatly impaired of their colours and other defaults to great slander and undoing of them, for which cause it is ordained and asserted that from that time forward no manner man of the same craft do dye no such cloth nor wool but if he be presented to the masters aforesaid that shall be for the time that he is good able and sufficient learned in the said craft upon pain to lose to the mayor and bailliffs to the use of the chamber and to the commune profit at the first fault the second fault the third default and for every default after the said three defaults without any forgiveness so that the said masters the third part coming of the said defaults shall have for their travail to their light provided always that all manner burgesses of this town may do here profit for to dye in their own houses their own proper clothes as it hath be used afore this this ordinance notwithstanding.

Item for the better governance of the said craft we the mayor sherriff bailliffs and commune council aforersaid have ordained and granted to the said masters and burgesses of the craft to for seide and to their successors for evermore that every master of the said craft of dyers when he hath dyed any cloth and after such dyeing is put to the towker to be rebbed that 4 maisters of dyers being for the time from this time forward may oversee all the defaults of every such cloth having in perche or on logges and in other lawful places of the working in dyeing of the same cloth without any letting or disturbing of any of the towkers or any other in their name and if they find in dyeing thereof of any defaults and will not present it to the court aforesaid that every master shall pay 40d that is to say 20d to the commune profit and 20d to the contribution of the said craft without any mitigation and if any person were the said masters or any such person so disturbing shall be amerced in 11d to be paid as it is aforesaid

Item when the merchants of the said town taketh their woad to the dyers to be set and there upon shall come and make report thereof that the masters of the said craft that shall be for the time be your authority and power may when all the masters and journeymen of the same craft to come togethe to a certain place assigned by the said 4 masters to commune thereof the same setting and of the making of the said woad and to ordain that one manner of woad of every merchant of beyond may be set at one assay and reported and in case that master after that he is warned by the said masters will not come to the place by them assigned in the manner aforersaid that then every such master shall be amerced in 20 d the one half to the mayor and bailliffs to the use of the commune profit of the same town and the other half to the said craft without any forgiveness. And if any journeyman after that he is warned by the masters come not to the place by him assigned in the manner and form aforesaid, that he then be amerced in 12d that is to say in 6d to the use of the common profit and vjd top the said craft without any forgiveness provided always that the said 4 masters and their servants all and singular occupying the said craft shall be ready to make reports of all such woad by him set to every merchant of the said town at his need, paying for their labour as it hath be used of old time upon the pain aforesaid to be raised in the manner and form aforesaid without any pardon

Latin translated – And after that all and singular the ordinances and articles above written had been read through there before the said mayor, sherriff, bailliffs and good men at the supplication of the said suppliants, it was seen and considered that all and singular these ordinances were useful both for the commonalty of the said town and for the craft of their common assent and consent they ratified and confirmed them so far as in them lay; and further they ordained that the aforesaid suppliants in the name of all and singular the craft shall have these ordinances newly made and ordained by us together with the ordinances and articles above said reduced to writing and fortified with the common seal of the the town of Bristol and enrolled in the red book of the same town among the ordinances of other crafts that they might appear on the record to those resorting again to hear these ordinances, full authority and power being always reserved to the mayor, sherriff, bailliffs and good men and their successors to revoke, annul, augment, make new or diminish the aforesaid ordinances or any of them as often as and whenever it shall seem expedient to the aforesaid mayor, sherriff, bailliffs and good men and their successors for the common utility, honour, and better government of the aforesaid community.

In testimony whereof our common seal of the said town of Bristol is appended to these presents.

Dated in Guildhall of Bristol, Wednesday, 14th Sept.1439

3) Act of Queen Elizabeth 1 prohibiting the use of logwood 1567

Anno vicesimo tertio Reginæ Elizabethæ
Cap. 1X Logwood and Blockwood shall not be used in the dying of cloth, etc.
Whereas of late years there hath been brought into this Realm of England, from beyond the seas, a certain kind of Ware or Stuffe called Logwood, alias Blockwood, wherewith divers Dyers, Clothiers, Hatmakers and others, have and do die daily, divers broad Clothes, Kersies, Woolls, Pennestones, Bayes, Cottons, Hose, Yarn, Hats, Caps, Flannels, Dockadoes, Rashes, tuft Dockadoes, and other things, forasmuch as the colours made with the said stuff called Logwood, alias Blockwood is false and deceitful, and the Clothes and other things wherewith dyed, are not only sold and uttered, to the great deceit of the Queen's loving subjects within this her Realm of England, but also beyond the Seas, to the great discredit and slander, as well of the Merchants, as of the Dyers of this Realm.

    For reformation whereof, be it ordained, enacted and established, by the Queen our Soveraign Lady, and by the assent of the Lords Spiritual and Temporal, and the Commons in this present Parliament assembled, and by the authority of the same, that all such Logwood, alias Blockwood, in whose hands soever the same shall be found, after the Feast of St. Michael the Archangel next ensuing, shall be forfeited, and openly burnt by authority of a Mayor or other head officer of the City or Town Corporate, or of two Justices of the Peace of the County where it shall be found, and that from and after twenty days after the end of this session of Parliament, no person of what degree soever be he, shall dye or cause to be dyed any Cloth, Wooll, or any other of the Premisses above mentioned, or anything whatsoever, with any of the said Ware or Stuff called Logwood, alias Blockwood, upon pain that the Dyer of every such thing so dyed, the one moiety to the use of the Queen's Majesty, her Heirs or Successors, and the other moiety to him that shall sue for the same, by action of debt, bill, plaint, or information, in any Court of Record, in which suit, no essoyne, protection, wager of Law, no writ of privilege for the defendant, shall be admitted or allowed; and the party offending, being thereof convicted, to remain in prison without bail or mainprize, till he have satisfied the same value.

    And where Clothes, Kersies and Hosen have been dyed with a colour which is commonly called a galled or mathered black, or a colour commonly called shoomake (sumach) and mathered black, which colours although they carry a shew of a good, true and perfect colour of woaded and mathered black, if of those as do buy the said colours, either in Cloth, Kersie or Hose taken so to be notwithstanding in proof and wearing prove contrary to the great deceit of the Queen's subjects, and discrediting of the Cloth and other things so dyed; for reformation thereof be it enacted, that no kind of Cloth or Clothes, Kersies, Bayes, Frisadoes, broad or narrow, hosen or other things, being in the nature of Cloth, shall from henceforth be mathered for a black except the same be first grounded with Woad onely, or with woad and a nele, alias blew Inde, unless the madder be put in with Shoomake (Sumac) or Gallis and that from and after twenty days from the end of this Session of Parliament no person of what degree soever, be he shall dye or cause to be dyed any Cloth or other things abovesaid of what kind or nature soever, mathered for black, not having a grond of woad onely, or of woad and a nele, alias blue Inde, unless the madder be put in with Shoomake (Sumach) or gallis, upon pain that the Dyer of every several thing so dyed, the one moiety thereof to the use of the Queen's Majesty, her Heirs or Successors, and the other moiety to him that will sue for the same, by act of debt, bill, plaint or information in any Court of Record, in which suit, no essoyn, protection, wager of Law, no writ of privilege for the defendant, shall be admitted, or allowed, and the party offending being thereof convicted, to remain in prison, without bail or mainpize till he have satisfied the same value.

Provided always, that it shall and may be lawful to dye all manner of galle black, shoomake black, alias plain black wherein no madder shall be used, as heretofore hath been done: this, or anything therein contained to the contrary no withstanding.

Provided always, that every dyer that shall after the Feast of Pentecost next ensuing the end of this Session of Parliament, dye any of the said clothes, Kersies or Frisadoes mathered and not woaded, shall before he deliver any of the same forth of his hands, be a seal of lead to every of them, in which the letter M, signifying Mathered, shall be connected upon pain that every dyer offending to the contrary, shall forfeit for every yard of the said Cloth, Kersies, Bayes or Frisadoes mathered and not woaded, after the said Feast of Pentecost, and shall not first give notice to the buyer thereof, that the same is not woaded, shall forfeit also double value of all such cloth, Kersies, Bayes and Frisadoes, as he shall sell: which forfeitures shall to the party that shall sue for the same in any Court of Record, by action of debt, bill, plaint, or information, wherein no essoyn, protection, or wager of Law shall lie.

4) A proclamation prohibiting the export of wool except as finished cloth. 1606

(6th. April 1606)

By the King,

A PROCLAMATION
For the putting in Execution the Laws and Statutes of this Realm, for the Preventing the Exportation of Sheep, Wooll, Wooll-fels, Woollen-yarn, Mortlings, Shorlings, Wooll-flocks, Fullers-earth, and Fulling-clay out of this Kingdom.

JAMES R.

hereas not withstanding the good Provision made by divers Laws and Statues of this Realm ,prohibiting the Transportation of Sheep, Wooll, Wooll-fels, Woollen-Yarn, Mortlings, Shorlings, Wool-flocks, Fullers-earth, and Fulling-clay, out of this Our Realm of England,Dominion of Wales, or Town and Port of Berwick upon Tweed, or any of the Isles, Ports, Creeks or Places thereof, into the Realm of Scotland, or into foreign parts

beyond the Seas;By which Laws and Statutes, besides the pecuniary Penalties and forfeitures thereby imposed, such Transportation is declared a felony, not only in the Transporters thereof, but also in their Aiders and Abettors; and not-withstanding the several Proclamations of Our late Dearest Brother, and Ourself, in pursuance of the said Laws; divers persons evilly-disposed to the welfare of this Our Kingdom and Dominions aforesaid, presuming upon Our Lenity in not exacting the Penalties aforesaid, upon the lives and Estates of such Offenders, as by Law We might, have assumed to themselves, and do daily licenciously assume to themselves in Defiance of Us, Our Government and Laws aforesaid not only clandestinely, but by open force and Violence with Armed Companies of Men, the Liberty to Convey and Transport the Commodities aforesaid into parts beyond the Seas; and also to Rescue the same out of the hands and Possession of Our Officers of the Customs, and others acting in their Aid, when by vertue of Our Authority the said Commodities have been seized, and in Riotous and Tumultuous manner have beaten and wounded Our said Officers, and those acting in their Aid; We taking the same into Our Princely Consideration, and duly weighing the evil consequence thereof to the Staple Manufacture of Clothing in this Our Kingdom, have thought pursuant, by the Advice of Our Privy Council, and We do, by this Our Royal Proclamation, as well as in pursuance of the aforesaid Laws, as in vertue of Our Royal Perogative, streightly Charge, Prohibit and Command that no manner of Sheep, Wooll, Wooll-fels, Woollen-yarn, Mortlings, Shorlings, Wooll-flocks, Fullers Earth or Fulling-clay, be at any time or times hereafter, by any person or persons whatsoever, whether Natural-born-Subjects, Denizens or

Strangers, Exported, Transported, Sent or Conveyed out of Our Kingdom, or Dominions aforesaid, or any of the Isles, Ports, Creeks, or places thereof, into the Kingdom of Scotland, or into any foreign parts beyond the Seas, upon pain of Our highest Indignation, and the severest Penalties, which by the Laws and Statutes of this Our Realm may be inflicted upon the Offenders themselves, their Aiders, Procurers, Abettors and Labourers, their lives and estates. and We do hereby declare, That We will cause to be effectually put in Execution the Laws and statutes aforesaid, and will exact the Penalties accruing, as by Law We may. And We do hereby streightly Charge and Command all Our Officers and Ministers, as well Civil as Military, to be Aiding and Assuisting to Our Officers of Our Customs, and others duly Authorised to put in Execution the said Laws, and all others acting in their Aid.

Given at Our Court at Whitehall the Sixth Day of April in the Fourth Year of Our Reign. (6TH. APRIL 1606)

GOD SAVE THE KING

LONDON, Printed by Charles Bill, Henry..........Newcomb, Printers to the King's most Excellent Majesty.

5) Dyestuffs listed and used in 1548 in Italy

Archil	Persian Berries
Bitter almonds	Polish Cochineal
Black Alder	Saffron
Blackberry leaves	Sage
*Brazilwood	*Sticklac
Dyer's Alkanet	Sumac

Fenugreek
Genista tinctoria or Broom
*Indigo
Kermes or Grain
Madder
Oak galls
Pomegranate

Hedge mustard

*Turmeric
Walnut
Rue
redoul (Coriaria myrtifolia)
Weld
Woad
Young fustic (Cotinus coggrygria)

6) Chemicals in Medieval Dyeing 1448

1. Ashes of Hartshorne — Potash
2. Ashes of peach stones — Potash
3. Borax — Disodium tetraborate
4. The source for the dyers was usually the waste and sweepings of flour mills
5. Brass filings
6. Cinnabar — A bright red mineral form of mercury sulphide — Principle ore of mercury
7. Common oil — Olive oil
8. Common salt — Sodium chloride
9. Copper filings
10. Egg shells
11. Gum Arabic
12. Iron scale — Iron oxide
13. Iron sulphate
14. Lead filings
15. Linseed oil
16 Live lime — Quicklime or calcium oxide
17 Olive oil

18 Orpiment and realgar   A natural yellow mineral form of arsenic sulphide This was used both as a mordant and as a pigment[6]
19 Potassium carbonate
20 Roman vitriol   Iron sulphate
21 Sal ammoniac   Ammonium chloride - prepared by fractional crystallisation from a solution containing salt and ammonium sulphate, which occurs as the mineral
22 Sal niter   Saltpetre, nitre, potassium nitrate - occurs as a mineral in some arid regions
23 Soap   Originally made by boiling animal fats with soda (sodium hydroxide)
24 Soda ash   Sodium carbonate - can be prepared by crystallisation from any one of a number of natural deposits, such as natron which is a mineral form of hydrated sodium carbonate
25 Soot   Carbon
26 Steel filings
27 Sulphur   The element occurs in many sulphide and sulphate minerals. Native sulphur occurs in places such as Italy and Sicily
28 Tartar of wine   A crystalline naturally occurring carboxylic acid. It can be obtained from tartar (potassium hydrogen tartrate) deposits from wine vats. Also known as argol, argal or argil.
29 Urine   Stale urine was until about 1850 the only source of ammonia.
29 Verdigris   The composition varies depending on atmospheric conditions. Includes the basic copper carbonate, sulphate and sometimes chloride
30 Vinegar   dilute impure acetic acid
31 Wine

Wood Ash   Potassium carbonate

7) Medieval Dye Recipes

Dyestuffs of 16th. century Italy:-

alum	bran
brazilwood	indigo
kermes or cochineal or grain	madder
soluble iron salts (ferrouis sulphate)	Tartar
(potassium tartrate)	
urine or ammonia	vinegar
weld	vinegar
woad	gum arabic

List of medieval recipes

Red, Yellow, Blue, Green, Brown, Black

No.1 Yellow

A Modern instructions for yellow

Ingredients		
	Woollen cloth	2ozs
	Water	
	Alum	6gms
	tartar (potassium tartrate)	1gms
	weld	30 gms
	young fustet	0.3 gms

Method   First soak the cloth in water. Dissolve alum and tartar in water immerse cloth and boil for 30 minutes. Allow to cool, remove cloth and rinse in fresh water. Boil weld and fustic together for 30 minutes, strain and cool.

Immerse cloth and boil for 30 minutes. cool, remove and allow to dry.

No. 2 Safflower

A) For yellow dye. soak dyestuff in cold water made slightly acid with vinegar. Sqeeze dyestuff by hand to extract all yellow dye.

B) To obtain red dye .Squeeze dyestuff to reduce water then add washing soda and knead like bread. add water to extract red dye. Repeat then add lemon juice to neutralise. Dye wet wool or silk in this.

No.3 To make wool a light red

Modern Instructions
    Ingredients

Woollen cloth	2ozs
Water	
Alum	38 gms
cochineal	7 gms
Madder	23 gms
Lime water	0.3 pints

    Method

Mordanting – Dissolve alum and cochineal in water, heat it if necessary to dissolve it. Next add the woollen cloth to the tepid mordant liquor, bring to the boil for 2 hours and allow to cool for 3 hours until just tepid. Remove wool and rinse in fresh cold water.

Dyeing – Place madder and the lime water to the mordant liquor while it is tepid. Stir well, add the cloth and keep stirring to ensure even pick up of the dye and heat for 10 minutes, **but do not boil**. Allow to cool, remove the cloth and hang up to dry.

Alternative add brazilwood for deeper colour

No 5 Blue

indigo and sod. dithionite

Method ½ teaspoonful of indigo and 1 teaspoonful of sodium dithionite in 3 pints of water. Warm to tepid temperature. Wait 20 minutes for indigo to dissolve to greenish colour. Wet cloth and immerse for 10 minutes.

No 6   Green

This can be done by immersing yellow cloth in indigo pot or immersing blue cloth in yellow dye pot.

No 7 Brown

Modern instructions
Ingredients Cloth   2ozs

　　　　　Water
　　　　　ground gallnuts　　27 gms
　　　　　gum arabic　　　　8 gms

Method Add galls and gum arabic to water and heat up and boil to dissolve. Cool, immerse wet cloth and bring to the boil. Boil for 2 hours.

No 8 Black wool

Modern instructions
Ingredients　cloth　　　　　　　　　　　　　　2ozs
　　　　　　German vitriol (iron sulphate)　　27 gms
　　　　　　alum of lees (potassium tartrate)　9 gms
　　　　　　alum　　　　　　　　　　　　　　9 gms
　　　　　　vinegar

Method Warm up a pot of water and vinegar. Add the iron sulphate, tartrate and alum to dissolve. Stir. When it is nearly boiling add wet cloth, stir and boil for 2 hours. Cool and rinse.

No 10 Brazilwood red

Modern instructions
　　Ingredients
　　　　　　　cloth　　　　2ozs
　　　　　　　water
　　　　　　　brazilwood　25gms
　　　　　　　Alum　　　　3gms
　　　　　　　vinegar

                ammonia
Method   Soak brazilwood and alum in vinegar for 24 hours. Soak the cloth in this and bring to the boil and add ammonia. Dry and rinse well in fresh water.

No 11   Red dyeing on thread, skeins, or linen

Modern Instructions
Ingredients
2 ozs of woollen cloth
Ground galls 10 gms
Mordant – boil 20 grams of ground galls for 10 minutes, cool, add cloth and boil 30 minutes, cool.Remove cloth. Add brazilwood and boil 30 minutes, cool. Decant liquid to remove wood bits. Add cloth and boil 10 minutes. Cool and dry

---

References
1 Le Monde des teintures naturelles, Dominique Cardon, pub.Belin 2003, ISBN 2 7011 2678 9
2 The Art of Dyeing in 5he History of Mankind, F.Brunello,1968
3 The Woad Plant and its Dye, J.B.Hurry, 1930
4 Madder Red, R.Chenciner, 2000, ISBN 0 7007 1259 3
5 Colour,Travels through a Paint Box, Victoria Finlay,2002, ISBN 0 340 826 320

End Notes

1 A chronology based on that published in the Encyclopedia Britannica.
2 Victoria and Albert Museum, Dept. orf Textiles, Catalogue of Tapestries by A.F.Kendrick, 1914
3 The Plictho by Gioanventura Rossetti,1548. Translated by W.M. Edelstein &H.C.Borghetty, MIT Press 1969
4 The Merchant of Prato, Iris Origo, Penguin Books1992
5 England's Apprenticeship 1603-1763, C.Wilson,1965
6 Chaucer in Modern English, John Edmonds To be published 2004
7 Early Decorative Textiles by W Fritz Volbach 1969
8 The Merchant of Prato, Iris Origo, Penguin Books1992
9 A History of Watchett, A.L.Wedlake, Exmoor Press 1955
10 Reading University Papers
    1) John P., Padden, A.N., Dillon, V.M., Kokubun T., Collins M.D., Alvarez N., Hutson R., Edmonds J., Hall A.R., Compton R.G., Perkin S.J., Gamblin D. P., Davis J., Marken F. (2000). Solubilization of indigo using Clostridium bacterium, *Fourth Int. Symp. On Natural Colorants*, San Diego, California,2-5 April 2000, organised by The Hereld Organisation.
    2) Kokubun T., Edmonds J., John P. (1998). Indoxyl derivatives in woad in relation to medieval indigo production. *Phytochemistry*, 49, 79-87
    3) Padden, A.N., Dillon, V.M., John P., Edmonds J., Collins M.D. (1998). Clostridium used in Medieval Dyeing. *Nature* 396.225
    4) Padden, A.N., Dillon, V.M., Edmonds J., Collins M.D., Alvarez N., John P. (1999). An indigo-reducing

moderate thermophile from a woad vat, Clostridium isatides sp. nov. *Int. J. Of Systematic Bacteriology*, 49, 1025-1031

5) Padden, AN, John, P, Collins, MD, Hutton, R and Hall, AR (2000). Indigo reducing *Clostridium isatidis* isolated from a variety of sources, including a 10th – Century Viking dye vat. Journal of Archaeological Science 27, 935-956